FLYING THE FLAG

By the same author:

Woman Up – Pitches, Pay and Periods:
The Progress and Potential of
Women's Football

FLYING
THE FLAG

The Footballing Heroines of
the Home Nations Who Made
History abroad

Carrie Dunn

HERO, AN IMPRINT OF LEGEND TIMES GROUP LTD
51 Gower Street
London WC1E 6HJ
United Kingdom
www.hero-press.com

First published by Hero in 2025

Printed by Akcent Media, 5 The Quay, St Ives, Cambs, PE27 5AR

ISBN: 9781917163538

Prologue: Raising the Flag   3

PART ONE   9
Survivor   11
Challenger   39
Learner   67
Master   89
Flier   107

PART TWO   121
Supporter   123
Settler   133
Wanderer   151

PART THREE   179
Latecomer   181
Manager   211

Epilogue   229

Acknowledgements   237

References   241

TO FOUR OF MY FAVOURITES:
CHRIS, DAVID, DIANA, SAM

THANK YOU FOR YOUR SUPPORT AND YOUR
FRIENDSHIP, AND FOR ALWAYS LISTENING
TO MY FOOTBALL STORIES.
EVEN WHEN YOU DIDN'T WANT TO.

FLYING THE FLAG

DRAMATIS PERSONAE

(IN ORDER OF APPEARANCE)

Jeannie Allott: England → Netherlands

Janice Lyons: England → Italy

Edna Neillis: Scotland → France, Italy

Kerry Davis: England → Italy

Sian Williams: Wales, England → Italy, USA

Vanessa O'Brien: England, Wales → Australia

Ann Gourley: Northern Ireland → Australia

Naz Ball: Wales, England → Germany

Lou Waller: England → Finland

Karen Farley: England → Sweden

Issy Pollard: England → Sweden, USA

Sammy Britton: England, Scotland → Iceland

Dan Murphy: England → USA

Ellen Maggs: England → USA

Pauline Hamill: Scotland, England → Iceland, Saudi Arabia

Michelle Barr: Scotland, England → USA, Iceland

PROLOGUE: RAISING THE FLAG

For every superstar female footballer earning a living from her skill, there are thousands of others who have spent thousands of pounds of their own money purely for a chance to play the game.

Take, for example, Mary Earps, part of the wonderful Lionesses squad who won the UEFA Women's Euros in 2022. Her attitude and her humour are appealing to many fans, especially young women, and it was no wonder people were delighted when she was named BBC Sports Personality of the Year in 2023. She is now a household name, and secured a high-profile move to European giants Paris Saint-Germain in 2024 – but when she was saving penalties in Women's World Cup finals in the summer of 2023, she was already thirty years old. She had been part of Manchester United's inaugural squad who competed in the Women's Super League in 2019, but many people may not know that she had spent time in Germany at the legendary VfL Wolfsburg prior to that.

And for those who follow women's football, it is verging on common knowledge that by the end of the 2023/24 season, Lucy Bronze had won five Champions League titles, three with Lyon in France, two with Barcelona in Spain. People may even know that she – like her younger England team-mates Lotte Wubben-Moy and Alessia Russo – spent her college years at the University in North Carolina, in the United States.

But do they know about the women who pursued a college education in the United States before the turn of the millennium?

Women's football has long taken a back seat in England. The Lionesses' success in successive summers in 2022 and 2023 grabbed plenty of attention, not least because there were no men's tournaments to distract from their achievements. The domestic Women's Super League is beginning to capture its own audience, but although many appear to think that its success has been a supernova, it has been a slow build; it has only been populated by solely full-time professional teams and players for a handful of seasons, and when it was launched, back in 2011, it was a closed league, with no relegation or promotion, and plenty of tight rules around contracts and salaries to ensure that top-tier talent was fairly distributed in an effort to guarantee a competitive spectacle. (Indeed, it is worth noting that longstanding global rules have defined a "professional" footballer as one who earns more than her basic expenses from the game – probably not the definition that most fans would come up with.)

Telling the stories of the women who played football prior to 2011 is crucial – not least because there were generations who were doing this in the face of what amounted to a wholesale ban. In 1921, the FA issued a memo to its member clubs telling them that football was a game "quite unsuitable for females" and forbidding them to allow women to play on their pitches. Where England led, other countries followed.

Yet women's football had been thriving prior to this. The famous factory teams of the Great War period – such as Dick, Kerr Ladies – attracted big crowds as they raised funds for war charities. Even earlier, the British Ladies, headed up by Lady Florence Dixie and captain Nettie Honeyball, had embarked on world tours, often opening people's eyes to the very concept that women could play football.

It is worth noting that even those women who were attracting big crowds were not necessarily also attracting positive sentiments. There were continual murmurs that playing football was not a ladylike activity, and that it could cause permanent physical damage to women; the usual concern was that it might prevent them from bearing children and taking up their proper domestic place. Many of these early players and teams were at pains to present themselves as traditionally feminine, and to show that they were not taking their sport too seriously, instead treating it as a novelty spectacle intended to raise money for good causes.

But, of course, many other women did take their football seriously, and the idea that they were no longer permitted to play was heartrending. And in many situations, those female footballers faced with the prospect of prohibition carried on regardless, playing wherever they could, often not even knowing that they had been banned until they tried to find a team – or, in the case of younger girls, until they tried to play for their school.

Even when the ban was lifted in the 1970s, the women's game in the UK remained resolutely amateur for decades, and essentially run by volunteers, albeit under the slightly more watchful eye of the official football authorities, both nationally and globally – who shunted aside the unofficial governing bodies who had set up international tournaments so that women could compete on the world stage, even if their teams and the matches were unsanctioned and would never appear in the formal record books.

It is no surprise that many, many talented women in Britain looked further afield for their footballing opportunities, seeking ways to play the game for a living, or to compete at the highest standard possible while combining it with another job or tertiary study, or to simply find a way they could contribute to improving the state of the game for other women and girls. For women, making a living as a professional footballer has historically been extremely challenging, with very few full-time roles available; often clubs overseas earmarked their limited budgets to pay a small stipend to their migrant players, but this has not always been enough for them to live on. The ways in which female footballers found possibilities away from the UK to make their love of their sport profitable while combining it with other work are many and varied.

Women's football in continental Europe took its first steps towards professionalisation two decades before the FA took full control of the game in England; in the USA, the law known by the shorthand term 'Title IX', guaranteeing equal funding for women's and men's sports in educational establishments, came into being in 1972, the first move towards making America the college destination of choice for aspiring female footballers. Indeed, even prior to this, one of the early stars of Dick, Kerr Ladies, Alice Mills, was so enamoured of the USA and the employment opportunities it provided her – in contrast to the depressed economics of the north-west of England – that she moved there permanently in 1924. One of her team-mates, Florrie Redford, seems to have represented France's Les Sportives the year prior to that.

Bearing in mind the limited press coverage of women's football even today, it's also no surprise that the adventures of the women who packed their boots and left the country have rarely been mentioned.

Up until now.

PART ONE

*Their game's been developed a lot longer than ours, their stand-
ard of play in the clubs is much better than ours, and we've
got to learn from that. That's what the girls should be aspiring
to play like... They've now got to go back and say we want to
play like the Germans and play as good as the Scandinavians.*
Ted Copeland, England manager, 13th June 1995

PART ONE

SURVIVOR

It looked like any other scrapbook, the record of a sporting career that began prodigiously early.

Each page was filled with clippings from local newspapers, eager in the 1960s to cover the story of a homegrown hero, gifted and charismatic from babyhood, made for the headlines.

The glossy photographs were interspersed with memorabilia from football superstars – a signed football from Bobby Charlton, a message to meet up with George Best for a media call, a note from Denis Law.

A curious reader would surely flick to the front, and gaze at the handwritten inscription: 'A story for Jeannie'.

The eight-year-old prodigy catching the eyes of reporters, fans and talent scouts alike was a little girl, playing football in England when women were still prohibited from stepping onto affiliated FA pitches.

The subject of this scrapbook did not get the worldwide superstardom her talent warranted, or that those legends of the game might have hoped for her. Yet her achievements are remarkable nonetheless, and most certainly never to be repeated.

⚽

Jeannie Allott always played football. It was something that drove her, something within her. Every breaktime at school, then every evening in the street, she would be out kicking a ball with her friends.

"At school, playtime, you had fifteen minutes – football in the playground," she remembered. "Then you got home at night, three o'clock, four o'clock – straight into the street playing football. You didn't have many cars in them days, and the bus used to come once an hour, so we used to move the goalposts [out of the road] – which were two jackets, or two plastic bags, or something. Every day, football, every day. I didn't know anything better."

She was good as well – better than the boys she played with – and she certainly stood out in the school team, not just because of her performance, but because of her blonde hair flying out around her as she ran.

Those long golden tresses were invariably mentioned in the news reports of the time, but the local sports scribes were not mentioning it to reiterate that this great player was a little girl, merely as a kind of curiosity, perhaps something for keen football fans to look out for should they be passing a park and see a group of children having a game – if they saw those flowing blonde locks, they knew they would be seeing something special.

Allott was certainly special. It was no wonder that she became something of a celebrity, not just in her town, but across the north-west of England. The *Chronicle*, from 6th January 1966, reported the premiere of new film *Billie* at the

Odeon Cinema, Crewe, with the headline 'Girl footballer as guest'. Nine-year-old Jeannie was the guest of honour, with the men of Crewe Alexandra mentioned very much lower down in the billing. Doubtless that was something to do with the film's plot: the adventures of a teenage girl who excelled at athletics. Yet it was also to do with Allott's burgeoning fame. She began to receive letters from all around the world, with one notable correspondent from India asking her to teach his children to play football. It was no wonder that famous names of the era were keen to meet her; she went to a special cinema screening with Manchester United's Bobby Charlton, who even gave her a box of chocolates, and his team-mate Denis Law sent her a pair of keepsake football boots. She later made a public appearance alongside George Best – "Apart from Elvis, the best-looking man I've ever seen" – and with the geographical proximity of Crewe plus the fashion for young men to grow their hair long, it is also not a surprise that one of Manchester United's coaches wanted to sign her for the youth team before realising she was a girl.

And it was certainly no wonder she was part of her primary-school football team, without question or hesitation. The photos of her with her peers exude joy – one shot is of Allott running down the wing, ball at her feet, a cardigan wrapped around her and a huge grin across her face; it seems clear that the boy coming into the frame in an effort to tackle her is going to find himself thwarted.

Allott too found herself thwarted, but not by any on-pitch rival. The scrapbook, kept lovingly for her by her mother, chronicles it faithfully: Crewe Schools FA forbade her from playing for Wistanton Green, declaring that girls were not eligible to play in their competitions. The school's headmaster, Mr Harold Morris, is quoted extensively in the press coverage, and from the modern vantage point he comes across as an impressive advocate, not just on Allott's behalf but for all girls wanting to play sport, urging the governing body to be "a little more broadminded". The gentlemen of the Crewe Schools FA, however, do not acquit themselves so well, with secretary Mr Bernard Travis quoted as saying: "It says in the rules that only boys shall play football and on these rules I shall make a stand against any girl playing football."

Mr Morris appears to have attempted a legal sleight of hand during these proceedings, saying that he had in fact written to the secretary of the English Schools FA – Crewe Schools FA's parent body – to discover the actual detail of these rules. He says that he had been advised that there was no explicit rule prohibiting girls from competing, but nonetheless girls would not be allowed to compete, in a maddening piece of circular logic.

After the arguments are exhausted – of course with the Crewe Schools FA getting their way – Allott herself peeps into the narrative, saying: "It has just not been my day today. I only got one mark in a test at school and then found that a pair of football boots I was to be given were the wrong size. Now this."

There is a glimmer in there of a wry sense of humour that has fully developed in the adult Allott. There is also evidence of a few more of Allott's defining characteristics, such as determination (verging on stubbornness) and a hint of rebelliousness, when the nine-year-old adds: "I love football and I hope my headmaster will still let me play in friendly matches."

Little Jeannie need not have doubted Mr Morris, who did indeed let her stay part of the school team set-up despite her very public official ban.

Of course, little Jeannie was not the only girl or woman having her footballing dreams crushed. As mentioned previously, in 1921, the FA Council had issued a memo to its members expressing disquiet over the reports received of women playing football, declaring the game "quite unsuitable for females" and telling clubs that they should not let women play matches on their pitches. As Allott's childhood exploits prove, the proclamations handed down from committees could only stop girls and women from playing on affiliated football pitches and in affiliated competitions; they could not stop girls and women from organising themselves or simply breaking the rules, which is what they did. When nine-year-old Allott was told of her ban, she tried out netball – a trial that lasted a handful of days before she returned to the football pitch, even if she was not allowed to compete officially, with Mr Morris, she thought, deliberately turning a blind eye.

Soon after the ban from Crewe Schools FA, Allott signed for Fodens Ladies – initially founded as a factory team in Sandbach sometime between the late 1950s to the early 1960s. Fodens were to become one of the most successful teams in

England during the 1970s, with the women who worked there benefiting from the company's attitude towards their staff's leisure time: they were keen to provide opportunities for art and music, with a new sports club opening in May 1963, although it was not initially expected that the female employees would be availing themselves of those facilities regularly. The exact year when the women's football team started has not been documented, but was somewhere between the mid-1950s and 1961; they soon moved away from being simply a works team and attracted players from elsewhere, such as Allott. She was playing alongside adult women, despite there being no available money at home to pay for necessary items such as football boots. Two men from Fodens had come to her house to invite her to join the club; she thought perhaps they had seen her in the local newspapers, or playing football in the street. They agreed that they would buy her boots and pick her up in the car every match day. When she was a few years older, she began to hitch-hike the six miles from Crewe to Sandbach for matches instead.

"I couldn't afford a train or anything," she said. "One day, I'll never forget, I saw this Rolls Royce. I thought, 'No, he's not going to stop.' He stopped."

A surprised Allott got in the luxury car and enjoyed the thickness of the seats – "You go over a bump, you don't feel anything!"

The driver told her he was not going the entire way to Sandbach, but that was fine by her as even a mile would get her closer to the pitch.

"Then he said, 'You know what?' I thought, 'Oh God, here we go.'

"'If you were my daughter, I'd smack your arse!' – because I was thumbing it. I said, 'Listen, mate, if you were my father, I wouldn't have to thumb it!' I had to get out straight away. I never forget that!"

She repeated his scolding: "Smack your arse?!" and laughed.

"Oh, I've been in everything: cars, lorries, milk carts. You name it, I've been in it, to get to bloody Sandbach. The good old days."

Allott herself is not a great hoarder of memorabilia. Looking around her cosy chalet home in Dordrecht, near Rotterdam in the Netherlands, the ornaments are such as one would expect to see anywhere – framed photographs of friends and loved ones, a clock, a couple of ashtrays for the roll-up cigarettes she smokes frequently. Then one glances to a sideboard placed next to a comfy leather arm-chair, and that is when one spots it – the so-called "legacy cap", the neatly tailored piece of scarlet velvet with gold trim and tasselling, with the number 10 embroidered at the centre, marking Allott's place in history – the woman who wore the number 10 in the official England team's first-ever match, making her the tenth name on the Lionesses roll of honour.

Not for Allott a display case for that cap, though, nor a special frame to protect it from any accidental damage. It is instead tossed casually, at a cheeky angle, over the top of a bottle of whisky.

The way Allott displays this token of her footballing career is apt. She – along with all the other women who played for England right from the start – never got given a cap as a memento during her playing career, something that their male counterparts did. The first official England team competed in 1972 a matter of months after the FA and its fellow governing bodies came to a consensus that their ongoing ban on women's football should be lifted, finding their hands forced more than a little by a string of successful events proving not just that women could and did play football, but that people wanted to watch it, and that companies wanted to invest in it. Perhaps the biggest blow to those who wished to uphold the ban was the unofficial international tournament held in Mexico and known as Copa 71, organised by the Federation of Independent European Female Football (FIEFF), operating completely separately from the men's established governing bodies, inviting six teams from around the world, which saw tens of thousands of people stream into the legendary Azteca stadium to support them. Though Harry Batt's British Independents were carefully not using the name 'England', with all the history and recent World Cup glory it connoted, others invariably used it to refer to them. On their return, this unofficial team, competing in an unofficial tournament, were punished severely by the Women's FA, the group of volunteers who had organised the women's game in England since the late 1960s, who were unsurprisingly keen to encourage some formal support from the FA for the women's game and desperate not to upset them any further. Their efforts paid off and the FA endorsed a women's team bearing the England name, even presenting them with a much-admired coach in Eric Worthington. He took his job seriously, running trials and inviting potential players along so that he could get to see them in action, and putting together the squad who faced Scotland at Greenock on 18th November 1972.

Jeannie Allott scored the winner that day in a 3–2 victory.

"I remember it was this field. It was hard as nails, it was just ice, you've never known anything like it... Normally the match wouldn't have gone on," she said. England had gone 2–0 down before coming back in the second half, and Allott's winner, she admitted, was more luck than judgement. She aimed to get the ball close to the Scotland goalkeeper and hope for a mistake, which was exactly what transpired. "It just bounced back into the goal."

Scotland had been the only European country who in 1971 had voted against lifting the ban on women's football when the continent's governing body UEFA had asked its members to include the game under their auspices. Though their team may have looked enviously at England – with their FA's eventual endorsement after half a century of enthusiastic elimination – Allott was scornful about the way she and her team-mates were treated. All she remembered being given as an England player was a white plastic bag, intended to carry kit, and she used it as a pillow to sleep at railway stations overnight when she had missed the last train home to Crewe from a match.

The FA's relationship with women's football remained tense. The Women's FA had been established in the decade before, run by volunteers and organising domestic competitions to the best of their ability without any official endorsement, and once the ban was lifted, they remained in charge of the women's game; they operated much like a county FA would in their geographical area, reporting ultimately to the FA but otherwise left to get on with it. Although the Women's FA were allowed to select a national side under the England banner, the resources upon which they could draw were extremely limited, beyond the services of coach Worthington, provided by the FA on a part-time basis alongside his responsibilities as a PE lecturer at Loughborough College (now University).

That lack of interest from the FA was reflected in broader society at the time. Allott vividly remembered how annoyed she got with the media coverage in England, recalling photographs of the team lining up for the national anthem that included only their legs, and offensive questions from reporters.

"What does your husband think about you playing football? Shouldn't you be in the kitchen? I just feel my blood boil!" she said.

She had only recently left school but was already losing interest in playing for England. Players were expected to attend trials to enable the head coach to pick his team, and Allott found it difficult to get motivated to play for a national team and association that she felt did not really want a women's team at all.

"I remember the last trial I went to, my grandad took me," she said, "and I just was not bothered. I thought, 'If I don't get picked, I don't give a toss; if I don't get picked, fair enough.'

"I didn't get picked. I did nothing on that field. I just didn't want to get picked for England any more, because it was a load of crap."

She knew that if she did get picked, the skeletal set-up would be the same, the scant resources would be the same, the lack of recognition would be the same, and she did not want to work that hard with no pay-off. Feeling that she was not valued by the FA, believing that the England team would never go forward and hating the media questions, Allott took a decision that changed her life. Her club Fodens had played matches against a Dutch side, Zwart-Wit 28 – "a good footballing team," she recalls.

"And there, everything was done for them. I thought, 'Ooh, that's not bad.'

"They'd go, 'Why don't you come over?'

"I thought, 'Well, nothing to lose, have I? I could always go back home if it doesn't work out.'

"So I went with another girl; her name was Tina. We both went out. I'll never forget my mum standing at the front door and I had my suitcase with me, and I said, 'Right, I'm off to Holland.'

"She said, 'See you next week.'

"I never went back home again."

Tina did not stay out there, but Allott did, playing for Zwart-Wit 28 and enjoying some of that luxury she had seen previously – people at the club making an effort to look after their players. She settled in straight away and never felt an ounce of homesickness, enjoying her football immediately and soon meeting Maria van den Elzen, known to everyone as Coby, the woman who would be her life partner. Of course, Allott still had a day job. After she had left school, she had started work at McCorquodale's, a big stationery factory.

"That was good money. I had so much money, I didn't know what to do with it. Just being as a kid having nothing, and then…" She stopped, considering the contrast between her childhood and finally having some spare cash of her own.

"I blew it all, of course!" she added with a cackle.

On arrival in the Netherlands, she worked in a sweet factory, then in a clerical office role, and finally settled into a role as a ship's planner, which she did for two decades: "That was brilliant. Manning all the ships, twenty-four hours a day work, but no matter. I enjoyed it."

Having that independent income was very important to her.

"At least I could pay my way, and I was playing football every weekend, so it was brilliant," she said. "I always looked after myself. I had a bit of money in my pocket. I thought, 'Why did in England you do all that lifting [hitch-hiking] and sleeping on stations? That will never happen again.' And it never happened again. And of course I met Cobes – that changed it completely."

Zwart-Wit were a good team, and even if they were not necessarily the best, the way the club operated was enough to keep Allott there. It was such a stark contrast to how she had had to strive to play when she was in England.

"When you had to go to a match, it was, 'Everybody in this car!' Nobody had to get on the bus or a train or whatever, or use your own money. Everybody got picked up. So just little things like that.

"'I've got no football boots!'

"'Oh, I've got a pair at home for you.'

"It was like a family – a family team."

That the Netherlands was such an attractive option may be surprising. The Dutch FA (KNVB) had been extremely negative about women's football when the first British teams began their publicity drives at the end of the nineteenth century, scorning the idea of the famous British Ladies playing the men of Sparta Rotterdam in 1896, with the outrage growing to such an extent that the proposed match was called off entirely. Yet the history of the women's game in the country ended up mirroring what happened in Britain, just on a slightly different timeline. Women's teams organised themselves in the first half of the twentieth century regardless of the lack of official approval. Men in power tried to stamp it out; Atria, the Dutch institute for women's history, reports that in 1935 the mayor of Amsterdam imposed a ban on women playing at all. In April 1955, an independent women's football governing body was established despite the scorn of the KNVB, and an unofficial national team was set up. When the KNVB finally acknowledged the women's game in 1971 – along with the other UEFA members in Europe – they were quick to take it within their remit, with 5,500 female players registered in that year. That was also the year that Zwart-Wit – a football club set up in 1928 – established their team for women.

Allott later moved on to KFC '71, based in Delft, roughly a half-hour drive outside Rotterdam, although she struggled to remember the exact dates of her time there. Although women's domestic football in the Netherlands was certainly in a better state than in England at that time, the historical documentation decades on was still relatively limited. A book celebrating ten years of KFC, published in 1981, did not include Allott's name in its honour roll of players; however, she was named in press cuttings in October of that year, suggesting that perhaps she joined the club sometime that summer. (Much to her frustration, she had been presented with a picture after her retirement, which did have the dates on, but which had peeled away with age, rendering it unreadable.) She had loved her time at Zwart-Wit, but reflected: "At the end of the day, it just wasn't for me. I wanted to go even higher."

The standard of play at Fodens had been excellent, and she wanted to be able to achieve her playing potential as well as having that off-pitch care that Zwart-Wit had offered.

"After a match we'd all go for a meal. You'd never go home walking or thumbing, somebody would always give you a lift, or bring you to the train station. It was just an absolutely fantastic team. We were champions of Holland. It was out of this world."

Some of her KFC team-mates became better known as top-class international coaches: Vera Pauw, who managed both Scotland and Ireland, and Sarina Wiegman, a double European champion with the Netherlands and England.

Wiegman and Allott were half of the quartet at the core of the KFC team, along with forwards Wil de Visser and Joyce Rontberg ("you couldn't get her off the ball!").

"This team, it was built on ball players – not bragging now," she explained. Not only that, they had their own bright yellow kit, and a sponsor who owned a takeaway restaurant, meaning the players got food as a treat after a good result.

"Sarina was a good footballer, technically. She was small. Against these Swedish girls and these French girls," Allott gestured above her own head, indicating the height of these opponents, "you'd think, 'Bloody hell,' but she was all right, she was a really good player."

The KFC '71 squad would finish training and go to the canteen for their refreshments afterwards, and Allott recalled that Wiegman – "quiet girl" – would sit in the corner with her parents, slightly separate from the rowdiness of the rest of the players.

"Oh, and never a swear word, Sarina!" added Allott. "At that age you could see she had her head screwed on. She knew what her plans were for the future. She's done well."

Allott even began an entirely new international career, picked to represent the Netherlands. There are certainly rules now around a footballer choosing the nation she wishes to represent at senior level; Allott doubted that anyone in either governing body knew or cared that she had previously played for England. However, none of her appearances for England were in sanctioned competitive tournaments, only friendlies, she said, so if anybody had objected that would be a defence. Never one to train hard – a naturally gifted player, she kept up her fitness simply because she played football so much – she did some training by herself in a local park when she joined KFC, and then had access to facilities once a week at the national complex in Zeist when she joined the Dutch squad. It was a one-and-a-half hour journey from her home to Zeist, but petrol costs were covered, so nobody was out of pocket for representing their country.

The Netherlands head coach was Bert van Lingen, with Dick Advocaat – later the men's head coach – taking charge briefly and leading the women to a win, much to his delight, in a friendly match against a boys' under-16 side. The coaching set-up and the relatively smaller number of players in the country meant that there was a scouting system in operation, and Van Lingen got a tip about Allott.

"They come to watch you," she said. "I didn't know he was on the [touch]line, and even if [I had], I don't give a toss. He was either going to pick me or not going to pick me, and I'm not going to do stupid things.

"I played a fantastic game. I was really good that game – not always good, but I was good that game! That's when I got picked. He said he was..."

She stopped, casting her mind back, but also searching for the right words in English after so long in the Netherlands.

"What's the English for when you're eating?... Drooling! He said he was drooling."

She retired from football in the middle of the 1980s, around her thirtieth birthday, and had no regrets at all. The Netherlands were planning a long-haul trip and she did not want to fly, instead deciding she may as well conclude her playing career.

"I achieved everything I wanted – played for England, played for Holland, I'd done it all," she said. "So that was time to stop. I thought, 'I'm not going on a football field and this eighteen-year-old girl's going to get the ball between my legs', you know, because you lose a bit of that speed, I think. No. It's time to stop."

It was still a young age for a footballer to retire.

"I'd got everything [that] I wanted, there was nothing more I could do, and then you settle down," she said, adding that she had had offers to play in other countries as a semi-professional. "I could have gone to Germany to play, paid football, I don't know how much it was. I said, 'Yeah!'"

When further details emerged, she learnt that the expectation was that she would work in a factory during the day, and play football in evenings and weekends.

"I thought, 'Nay.' Nay. I'm going to make my life here in Holland, I'm not going to go to Germany for a little wage and [work] in the factory making nuts and bolts."

Allott kept the promise she had made herself when she first arrived in the Netherlands – that she would never put herself through hardship again. She did not just mean stretched finances or physical discomfort, but also causing herself needless stress. She loved playing football, but she did not necessarily love the way that teams were run, and if it was making her unhappy, she would walk away. That was why she had left England, and it was why she decided to stop playing for the Netherlands as well.

"I remember being on this bus and we were going somewhere…we'd only just got on the bus and I thought, 'What am I doing?' because I wasn't happy. I thought, 'I'm getting off this bus and I'm going home.' I'd just had enough of the Dutch [FA], I'd had enough of England and the FA, and after a couple of years I just wanted to play football, I didn't want to play for the national team.

"'I have to be there, I have to do that' – I don't like that. If I know I'm playing Sunday at two o'clock in the afternoon, I'll be there, I'll get my kit on and I'll play football, and then I'll go straight home, but sitting on that bus, oh, it was awful, I don't know where the hell I was going. But that's just me, that's just me. If I don't like it, then I'll stop. They're not going to force [me] into anything if I don't like it. Football was my life and everything, but I'm not going to do anything that I don't want to do, whether that's for the national team or what. I don't give a toss."

In 2001, Allott was not feeling well. She had been having bad headaches but tried to ignore them, and she found her memory was deteriorating, making it hard for her to maintain her side of a conversation. She developed tremors, and then suffered a partial paralysis down the left side of her body, meaning her partner had to dress and care for her.

After an initial misdiagnosis of Parkinson's disease, she was then diagnosed with a brain tumour the size of an orange.

"I was having tests and tests, I was in the hospital in and out for months. Months!" she recalled. She took the news calmly, which in retrospect she attributed to the medication they had given her. She had to have a first operation to lift the skull away from the brain before the surgery to remove the tumour, and she remembered waking up in the intensive care unit and hearing a voice asking her a question.

"I remember this voice somewhere in the background saying, 'Who's the queen of Holland?'

"I thought, 'Who the bloody hell's that? I've just had a brain surgery! Who's the queen of Holland?!'

"Then I thought, 'Well, it's not Elizabeth. Hey, my brain's not bad! I can remember Elizabeth.'"

Though the doctors had not said that she had a genetic predisposition to it, she wondered whether it did indeed run in the family; her grandmother had died of shingles, which in retrospect she wondered may have been misdiagnosed, and her mother also died of a brain tumour. The doctors had also told Allott not to worry about her years of heading hard leather footballs, because they did not think that had caused it either, but she was unsure. After eighteen months of treatment, she recovered, but most of the other patients on her ward had died.

Her illness and recovery offered an opportunity for her to rebuild her fractured, fractious relationship with her father, at least. It also put an end to her famous, instantly identifiable long blonde hair.

"After my operation, because I had no hair or anything, I thought, 'Let's just clip it short,'" she said. "If you're sixty and your hair's down here," she gestured to her waist, "from the back you look, 'Wow!' And then you turn around and you're a bloody monument!" She grinned again. "So I thought, 'Let's keep it short.' And the blonde's gone now, unfortunately – grey!"

Half a century after Jeannie Allott made her England debut, her former KFC '71 team-mate Sarina Wiegman coached the new generation of Lionesses to European glory, winning the UEFA Women's Euros at Wembley Stadium. Wiegman and her players had been notably vocal not just about inspiring little girls to take up sport and to encourage those in positions of power to ensure girls had the same opportunities as their male peers, but to recognise the women who had fought for years to play football and who had laid the groundwork for the modern professional players to benefit. It would not be a huge stretch of the imagination to think that maybe Allott's story had stuck with Wiegman since their playing days.

Having lived in the Netherlands for the majority of her life, she was fluent in the language, and she was settled in her house in Rotterdam with her out-of-town retreat available for a touch more peace. Now retired, she kept an eye on an elderly neighbour and her pets; an animal lover herself, she kept a sack of seed in her car with which to feed any passing ducks.

Although she still defined herself as English, Allott's trips back to England were infrequent. She still refused to step foot on a plane, so any visits back to England now were done via rail on Eurostar, with the long boat trip from the port in Rotterdam a fallback option in desperate times. She loved to stock up on her favourite English foods – a particular brand of cheese-and-onion crisps, salad cream, pickled onions in malt vinegar (definitely not the silverskin variety) – although a new expat shop that had just opened up in Rotterdam meant less urgency to haul back carrier bags full of snacks. She spoke fondly of her nephews, the children of her sister, who entreated her to visit them in Devon; and she had made an overnight visit to the north-west of England to visit her brother, and to put flowers on her mother's grave. It was a far cry from Ivy Allott's prediction that Jeannie would only last a week out there, although her daughter had made an effort to keep in touch as best she could.

"I did come home once or twice a year, I must say. I wasn't too bad. I called her on some bugger's phone – I can't remember who it was – because she never had a phone, and I wrote letters, and no news is good news.

"'See you next week.' Oh, I'll never forget them words. Good old Ivy. Good old Ivy."

Allott returned to England in November 2022, when those first England players – the ones who had never been given a formal cap – were invited along to Wembley to watch a friendly against the USA. On what she described as "a night never to forget", they were presented to a near-sellout crowd, taking a sedate lap of honour around the pitch, having been given their legacy caps in a private ceremony earlier. Allott was pleased that she and her team-mates finally had an official cap, and the recognition from the game's governing body, but she felt that an acknowledgement on the pitch and a presentation behind closed doors was not enough. That was not because Allott was keen on self-publicity or on fancy ceremonies, but because she felt that the existence of the 1972 team and the years of failure to recognise their contributions remained an embarrassment, to be kept as hidden as possible. Maybe something more public might have appeased her, but maybe not. Really, there would be little that could make up for a half-century of neglect.

"Once that book's closed, it's closed, it's finished with me," she said. "Don't get me wrong, I like it when the FA invite the 1972 [players] to go down to London, I like that, but once I get back, it's closed for me."

She gestured at her phone, where she had been responding to a group chat with the other inaugural England players.

"These girls – best mates I have ever got. They thrive on these memories, and yeah, maybe I'm a little bit different. But what's happened has happened. They can't take it off me as long as I've got the memory, and no bugger else has to know."

What pained her particularly was knowing that her old Fodens team-mate Sylvia Gore – who scored that first official goal – had missed out on all this recognition, having passed away in 2016. Others from the squad were suffering from poor health and were unable to enjoy the occasions as much as they would have done twenty, ten or even five years previously. Of the original 1972 England team, Allott had always been the most outspoken, the most rowdily angry about the way she felt they had been ignored. Perhaps it was her physical distance that gave her the confidence to do that; no longer playing or coaching in England, she did not feel the need to couch her views diplomatically. Perhaps it was just Allott's personality, though; even had she stayed in England and continued playing for distinguished club sides such as Fodens, it is quite easy to imagine her continuing to call on the authorities to acknowledge their former failures.

She told the *Independent* in the summer of 2022: "Nothing that happened in the past should be forgotten, but the FA forgot us. We want a cap and I believe we deserve an apology."

Certainly the FA righted some of those wrongs by presenting those legacy caps. However, it is unsurprising that fifty years of anger and resentment do still simmer: not just the governing bodies, but the reporters who asked rude and intrusive questions, the photographers who took photos just of female players' legs, the continued attitudes that said that in England female footballers were not important or to be taken seriously.

"This is not to be forgotten, is it?" Allott said. "What we've all done, what we've all had to go through – go to other countries to get what you want. It's bloody awful that you have to leave your home country to get what you want."

Tim Allott – the son of Jeannie's sister – was born in 1974. All his childhood memories of his aunt were of her coming over from the Netherlands to visit; with no telephone in the house, the arrival of his "rogue" aunt, as he described her, was quite the occasion.

"We were quite an ordinary sort of family who didn't have much at home," he said. "So this little bit of glamour, if you like, came back to Crewe from this far-flung place called Rotterdam that I had never have seen and didn't know much about."

He and his brother Warren learnt of her footballing exploits from his grandmother; he later attended the same school that Jeannie had, giving him an additional connection with her. Yet even though he began to piece together what she had achieved as a teenager, even as an older child himself he did not realise that she was still playing football in the Netherlands.

"I have got memories of having the odd kickaround with her in in the road behind our house and noticing how she how quick she was, and how quick she was shimmying from side to side and really going for it," he said. "I thought, 'Gosh!' and I'm really quite amazed by that. As a twelve-year-old, say, in the mid-1980s, at that point, I just assumed all the football stuff was historical."

Even as an adult, it did not quite click.

"Even in my twenties and thirties I guess I didn't give it too much thought, just getting on with my own life. It's only sort of the more recent stuff has made me think a bit more about the timeline and what was happening then – what was I doing? How did it all fit in and how did she end up doing that?"

That "more recent stuff" included Jeannie's increased media profile, most notably her repeated public comments criticising the FA's failure to celebrate the first England teams.

"I almost wanted to say to her, 'Don't go too mad,'" said Tim. "It was like she was really fighting for it and still a bit cross. I was almost wanting to say, 'It was a long time ago now, just enjoy the moment.' But all the [1972] Lionesses were [angry], it's still something that hurt quite a bit."

It was Jeannie's nephews who put her back in touch with her 1972 England team-mates by a sheer stroke of luck; Warren, a painter and decorator, happened to be listening to Radio 4's *Woman's Hour*, which featured the team, and in which they said they had finally been reunited – all except for one.

"Straight away my brother got in contact – 'They're asking for Jeannie Allott on Radio Four!' I think I messaged her. Obviously she got in contact at that point."

Tim and Warren accompanied their aunt to Wembley in 2022, to see her awarded her legacy number and souvenir cap and do a lap of honour around the pitch. After leaving the stadium, the recognition continued.

"It was a little bit mind-blowing," he recalled. "Just when you thought it had all finished, leaving Wembley, there was a huddle of people run forward and saying, 'Can you sign this?'

"[I thought] What's going on here? It was quite bizarre. These aren't the current Lionesses. They are the ones from the 1970s!

"It just seems strange – seeing people running up to my auntie for a signature. I never thought I'd see that!"

Having enjoyed this unique vantage point, Tim felt that he had a new insight into his aunt's life and achievements.

"This time, I'm an adult, and I can observe it – Jeannie and her football that I never got to observe in the 1970s because I was either not born or just too young. So yeah, I think that's quite an amazing thing. It's brought me a little bit closer to her and the football."

Understanding just what his aunt had done in football, and the sacrifices she had made for it, still amazed Tim – now the father of a daughter himself. He found it difficult to imagine her emulating Jeannie – hitch-hiking across the country, sleeping at a train station, packing up her life and moving to a new country where she did not even speak the language.

"It was a different time and a different era," he said. "We're very proud of her. We've told lots of people over the years the legend of my auntie playing for England, but people nodded and it didn't really mean much. I guess it's only the last couple of years that people know what you're talking about now. It wasn't really a thing a few years ago.

"But I've always been proud of my auntie Jeannie."

Auntie Jeannie vividly recalled those kickarounds with her young nephews on her trips back from Rotterdam.

"I remember playing football with him!" she declared with a hearty laugh, before adding a fond swipe: "He's not a footballer!"

She was also touched to know that Tim had such fond

memories of her partner Coby, who passed away from cancer in 2013.

"They were absolutely mad about her," she agreed. "She was a really, really great person, really great person. But with everything comes an end, doesn't it? Just a shame that it was at [sixty-four]. Too early."

The two had played for Zwart-Wit together, with Coby a left-footed centre forward who had even played in West Germany earlier in her career. When Allott moved on to KFC, the two came up against each other, of course.

"We always won. Always. The last match, I'll never forget, was 12–1. She scored that one goal – OK, I'll give her her due!

"And that's how we started. That's how we started. Thirty-seven years together before she passed away."

Reunions with her old team-mates were an unexpected delight for Allott. When she had been trying to establish the years she had played for KFC, her old captain Wil de Visser had got in touch with her; although neither got any further with working out the dates of Allott's time at the club, they decided they would organise a get-together of all their colleagues.

"It's like the Lionesses for 1972 getting together – now we're going to try and get the KFC team together," she said. "It's bloody busy!"

The only regret she had stretched back into her childhood and classic British kids' television, and not receiving a *Blue Peter* badge, although the memory was fuzzy on whether she had actually appeared in the studio or whether they had made a film about her. Having said that, she had kept so little of her other gifts and memorabilia from that time, it is questionable as to whether she would have been able to keep it intact over the years.

"I remember Bobby Charlton giving me a football – a real leather white football with his autograph and everything. Don't know where they are, them football boots from Denis Law. I didn't keep anything. It was just play football and that was it. The shirts and the programmes, you got a little present – nay, I wasn't into that at all. Isn't that awful? It sounds as though I don't care."

Allott did care, but she treasured her past in the way she lived her life – in her own inimitable style. She glanced once more at her red legacy cap, placed at that askew angle over the bottle.

"The other girls, they've got everything – the shirts behind glass, the caps behind glass. I think it looks nice on that whisky bottle."

CHALLENGER

"I remember playing against Jeannie Allott!" recalled Janice Lyons. She had begun her career with Manchester Corinthians – the arch-rivals of Allott's former side Fodens, so she knew the best players by reputation. Besides, Allott's physical presence and appearance always made her stand out.

"Very... very..."

Lyons sought for the right word, and instead opted to explain her memory more fully. "She's a centre forward, isn't she? And she had long blonde hair.

"And she was so hard! Can I say that? A really hard player!"

Lyons grinned. It was evident that this was the highest of compliments.

"I was a defender – I was a full back, a right full back. But I remember her coming forward and she was like a powerhouse. And I had to tackle her! I was hard myself, but I just thought..."

She made a face, eyes widening.

"She was really nice. A good player. Had a tremendous shot on her. She deserved to play for England, she did."

Janice Lyons was a fine player herself, and any educated observer would have expected her to get international recognition. With no such thing as a girls' football team at her primary school in the 1960s, she first played as part of a boys v girls charity match on the housing estate where she lived, organised by the local publican to raise money for the survivors of the Aberfan disaster in October 1966, when colliery waste and wet weather combined to create a slurry that slid down the mountain and crushed and buried alive the village school, killing 116 children and 28 adults. It was a match played in the best of spirits for the best and most emotive of causes, but one young player took it seriously.

"I was everywhere," Lyons said. "I was so muddy, and everybody else – you could see all their football strips. I was the only one who was diving in."

The Alderley and Wilmslow Advertiser reported with a patronising if well-meaning tone: "Needless to say the boys won, but it could very well have been a victory for the girls, if the boys had not formed a barrier around the goalmouth and stopped the ball getting past." They also reported something Lyons herself did not mention – fondly nicknamed "Tiger", she was "hero of the match" for scoring or assisting all three of the goals scored by the girls, and was carried off the pitch in glory at the end of the match.

Enthusiasm is one thing, but playing ability is another, and it was apparent that little Janice was also a naturally skilled footballer. When her mother saw in the *Manchester Evening News* that the Manchester Corinthians were looking for new players, she took little Janice along to two trials before the team manager wrote them a letter inviting her to join them permanently.

That was in February 1968, and Lyons was very proud to represent the Corinthians, a club that grew out of the hotbed of women's football in the north-west, thriving after the Second World War, and capitalising on the interest in the sport from women following England men's 1966 World Cup triumph. Manager Percy Ashley had originally simply wanted to give his daughter Doris a team to play in, and he began to build a club to that end, attracting gifted players from good teams in the area and further afield. His Corinthians travelled and impressed the world, and it was here that Lyons began her footballing adventures.

When Corinthians went to France for a four-team tournament in Reims in July 1970, it was Lyons's first time on a plane. Team manager Gladys Aiken had insisted on each player being measured up for a skirt suit to wear on their travels; "We all had suits, with a little badge, and a white shirt, and a nice skirt, because the manager wanted us to look professional and look like ladies – which we did do," said Janice.

The Corinthians squad shared a dormitory, and were on the same floor as Italian team Juventus.

"Imagine what went on!" exclaimed Lyons. "It was so good. We was on one side and they was on the other, and it was little blocks, separated blocks, but we could shout over and we used to have to go through their bit to go to the toilet and the shower. So we made some really good friends with the Italians in that tournament – which we won."

Lyons and her team-mates stayed in touch with some of

the Juventus players, writing letters and spending holidays with each other. On one visit, she joined in a training session with the squad, and was invited to stay on and play for them.

She was seventeen at the time.

It is easy to understand why Juventus made the offer to Lyons, young as she was. The path from England to Italy was already in the process of being created – primarily by Sue Lopez, born in 1945, who had already set up tentative links with the country and joined Roma in 1971, but whose name had been synonymous with women's football in Southampton from the 1960s onwards. Seven teams – including Lopez's Royex – joined together to form the South Hants Ladies' Football Association (Southampton and District) League, with the first fixtures played in September 1966 on Southampton Common. Women's football researchers for years to come will benefit from Lopez's 1997 book *Women on the Ball*, part history, part autobiography, in which she recalls the state of facilities on that opening day and for years to come: three pitches with goalposts but no nets, wooden changing huts, a toilet and an outside tap to wash off muddy boots. Compared to many women's teams who have fought to find places to play since the 1921 ban and onwards, even to the current day, the toilet facilities and running water may sound like veritable luxury.

Intriguingly, Lopez makes it clear that she and her team-mates had no idea that women's football was still formally banned by the powers-that-be, and that men who were coaching women's teams were running the risk of a ban themselves if their activity had been uncovered. She chronicles the creation of the Women's FA in 1969, and inaugural secretary Patricia Gregory's letter to her local newspaper asking whether there were any teams she would be able to join; after the success of England's men at the 1966 World Cup, girls and women across the country wanted to give the game a go themselves, and they had no idea about any FA memorandum from half a century previously that judged the sport "unsuitable for females". Perhaps it was the lingering sense of football's "unsuitability" for women that led to the neglect of players' safety and fitness; the league acknowledged a concern around injuries but did not recommend a first-aid kit on each team's bench along with a qualified trainer, instead sending clubs a letter warning players that "over-eagerness" in any sport was likely to cause injury. Lopez sustained a severe concussion in one match and received no suitable treatment at the time. When she sought medical treatment herself, her doctor told her to take up a sedentary sport such as fishing. Again, the lack of understanding of head injury and the possible long-term consequences both continue to be a problem in modern-day sport.

Lopez was part of the first Southampton women's team, essentially a representative team from the Southampton and District League, who played their first challenge match against Paulsgrove Ladies on 11th December 1966. It was due to be hosted by Sholing FC, until the Hampshire FA prevented it due to the continuing prohibition on women playing football on official football pitches. The match was switched at the last minute to the Southampton Sports Centre, and a new footballing dynasty on the south coast was born.

In 1969, Lopez was part of an English XI that travelled to Turin to take part in the Federation of Independent European Female Football's invitational Italian Tournament – an early and unofficial form of a women's European Championship. Led by Chiltern Valley's manager Harry Batt, the squad consisted mostly of his own players, plus five from Southampton. With no support or recognition from the FA, the players themselves spent their journey to Italy – via train and ferry, not via air – sewing Union Flag patches on to their tracksuits in an effort to make them look like a unified national side. The English team finished third, and Lopez recounts the thrill she felt to play in real stadia, in front of thousands of spectators, and taken seriously by the tournament organisers as well as the media, adding that she personally relished the atmosphere, enthusiasm and friendliness she felt there.

It was the first step towards a monumental move. Marco Rambaudi, president of Real Torino, spoke to Lopez and invited her to train with his squad. She agreed, staying on in Turin after the rest of the English squad had gone home, and playing in a friendly match before heading back to Southampton herself. The newspapers in Italy and back at home began reporting that Lopez was set to agree a professional deal with one of the Italian clubs. Indeed, Real Torino wanted her to return to Italy and sign what she describes in her book as a "full-time contract", but after eighteen months of indecision she decided to sign instead for Roma in May 1971. In a later interview, Lopez said that Torino had not been specific enough with their offer, while Roma made a good case which included travel and accommodation – although, it is worth pointing out, she does not mention any additional salary payment. She was adamant that she was never paid for playing football.*

Simultaneously, the Women's FA was finding its footing and attempting to come to a collaborative agreement with the FA, with the hope of being able to field an official England team rather than Batt's invitational squad. The Women's FA, run entirely by volunteers, obtained funding from organisations such as the Sports Council which was reliant on their participants being completely amateur. Female footballers were made well aware that if they gave up their amateur status, they would be subject to a ban, because they would also be jeopardising the status of women's football as a whole as it made its first tentative moves towards a genuine domestic competition; indeed, Lopez even notes this in her book, later observing that she had been the first in a steady trickle of women from Britain who were "willing to risk being banned" as they sought to push themselves to their playing peak in a challenging yet supportive environment. It is easy to understand the allure of Italy: the first country they knew of that had a genuinely competitive nationwide league for women, the Federazione Italiana Calcio Femminile (FICF), with investment and

* Williams, *Globalising Women's Football*

sponsorship for competitions and for clubs, it was all very different to what was happening in England.

Lopez made her debut for Roma on Sunday 23rd May 1971 against the previous season's league runners-up Piacenza, coming on from the bench for the second half and scoring a late consolation goal in a 2–1 defeat. She had resigned from her job in the UK as a secretary, which she describes as an easy decision: "Nothing could ever beat playing football full-time." Yet she is at pains to point out that she was not paid to play football, but received only living and travelling expenses as she shared a flat outside the city with another player. She speaks of the day jobs of her Italian team-mates, one working in a pizzeria, one a wigmaker, one caring for an invalid mother. She mentions hearing from a British sports writer, Brian Glanville, that two Fiorentina players were receiving £40 a week in wages to play for their team (roughly the equivalent of £700 in 2024). This may not sound like a lot, but Hansard, the parliamentary record, indicates that at that time the average man in manual work earned just over £28 per week. Kevin Keegan, about to become a legend at his new club, signed for Liverpool in May 1971, just as Lopez was moving to Italy. His autobiography reports that manager Bill Shankly initially offered him £45 per week in wages, and ultimately agreed on £50 per week. If those Fiorentina players were receiving £40 per week, that was a very sizeable salary both for the time and for the game.

The Roma players did not have to pay anything to play football, such as a club membership subscription; again, players having to cover many of their own expenses has historically been very common up to the current day, even in the upper echelons of women's football. Lopez is hazy on the specifics of where the money came from to cover their costs. Gate receipts may have been part of it, but, as she suggests, in a country where independent international women's football tournaments had enjoyed such success, it is likely that some savvy businesspeople were choosing to invest their money in the sport. One of the schemes they chose to spend their money on was a tour to the USA, where Southampton were one of their opponents, on Lopez's suggestion. The players got on well and some stayed in touch, and when one visited one of her Italian counterparts, the then-Southampton manager suspected that she was considering a transfer. He wrote to Lopez informing her that the Women's FA were looking into this so-called "poaching" by Italian clubs, and warned her that it was commonly thought that she was a paid professional for Roma – should she return home, she would need to be able to prove that she had always remained an amateur if she wished to participate in WFA competitions.

In January 1972, Lopez played in the Coppa Italia final, helping Roma to a 1–0 victory over Fiorentina, and then returned to England. She intended to go back to Italy and resume her career with Roma, but found herself instead embroiled in the tail end of Southampton's season. Then she discovered that the Women's FA were setting up an official, sanctioned England team and understandably wanted to be part of it, and part of moving English women's football on to the next level. Even players who only received expenses were at risk of being judged as non-amateurs and thus not eligible for consideration. So Lopez decided to stay in England, although she missed out on the first national team trials after breaking her ankle in a friendly match against a men's side.

⚽

Janice Lyons, however, had no such qualms about what might happen in the future. With an offer from Juventus on the table, she sought advice.

"The manager of Manchester Corinthians told me, 'If you go to Italy, you will not play for England.' That's really bad, isn't it? So it's a big choice to make. But I went."

The Corinthians manager was not wrong. Lyons never got picked for England, but equally she never really considered turning Juventus down.

"I was so enthusiastic, and wanted to live my dream, and I wanted to play in Italy. So I thought, 'Well, if I can't play [for England]…' Because you were up against a lot of competition by then, and I don't know if you realised it, but there was a still north-south divide as well, there definitely was, so a lot of people from Southampton and the Midlands were picked for England, even though there was tremendous players playing up north like [at] Fodens – apart from Jeannie Allott, by the way [who did get selected] – and Manchester Corinthians, there was still a divide.

"So I thought, 'Well, I might not get in the squad, you know, let alone play.' And I wanted to do it because if I hadn't taken that choice, I would never have gone to Italy.

"It was the only opportunity, I thought, to go there. Nobody did that then, hardly. I mean, Jeannie went to the Netherlands, I know that. I went on my own to Italy, I wanted to go, but that's what I was told: 'You won't play for England', and I didn't play for England."

Lyons had got the travel bug with Corinthians, and it was something that stayed with her. She returned home from her holiday in Italy and told her – unsurprisingly quite shocked – parents that she was going to go and play for Juventus.

"I said to my mum, 'I'm going to play in Italy.'

"She said, 'What?'

"'I'm going to play in Italy.' There was nothing in the world that was stopping me, because it didn't then.

"It was very unusual, don't get me wrong, for somebody to just to do that, at that time, in 1973, 1972.

"And she said, 'Well, you're eighteen in September, I can't really stop you, even though I don't want you to go' – not that that bothered me, because I was going anyway."

With hindsight, Lyons knew she could have handled it more carefully with her parents, but attributed her single-mindedness to her youthful lack of fear. She had no second thoughts about giving up her job either. After passing her exams at school she had got a position at the Midland Bank, certainly a highly regarded role and one that offered a career path.

"You worked your way up," said Lyons. "I was training to be a cashier at the time I left. I just found it so boring.

"I gave that up. I thought it wasn't the career for me, really, because you was forced to go into jobs then and you didn't really have a choice of jobs. They put you in blocks: 'Well, because of your exams, you can do this, or that – you can join the government, civil service, or you can go in a bank.'

"I didn't know at the time what I really wanted to do. I wish I would have gone [into] further [education], but if I'd gone into further education, you see, I wouldn't have gone to Italy because I'd have been doing other things."

So Lyons handed in her notice and headed off. The travel was not entirely straightforward. With no direct flights from Manchester to Turin, Lyons flew to Paris and then took a scenic if circuitous train ride through the Alps to her new home, arriving at day break, and was met at the station by her friend and new team-mate, Valeria, with whom she stayed in the town of Ivrea for her first days in Italy. She had to register her arrival, using her birth certificate as her identification document, and then underwent and passed her physical medical at the main club training ground.

The club president was keen for his new international signing to live closer to the centre of Turin, and got her booked into a women's hostel run by nuns. It was a busy pension, populated mostly by young women from all over the country travelling to the city to seek work. Bedrooms were shared, and the meal times were both hectic and noisy. Lyons did not speak a word of the language she was hearing all around her, but picked it up quickly.

"I was learning all sorts of phrases and swear words which they told me! They had a bit of banter with me – they was telling me things that were swear words but I didn't know they were swear words!" It led to an unfortunate incident where Lyons went to get her serving of dinner from the nuns on duty and, given a script in Italian by her mischievous pals, ended up offending them with an obscenity. Fortunately, the nuns were wise enough to know that both they and Lyons were the butts of the girls' joke. Lyons loved her time at the hostel.

"It opened up a whole new world for me, really, you know, meeting different people and cultures," she said.

Of course, playing for Juventus also gave her many more opportunities. First, her footballing experience was enhanced by a much more rigorous and professional approach to training. The squad trained twice a week and played on Sundays – very different from the more slapdash set-up she had been used to in England.

"They put a particular emphasis on diet – what we should be eating," she said of the squad's trainers. "I mean, in England, you just didn't have that. They do now, but they didn't then, so there was so much influence on what we was eating – health-wise, nutrition-wise, making sure you get the correct food and drink."

She also enjoyed travelling around Italy, joining the rest of the squad on a special coach to take them to their away games.

"I love Turin, but I've been all over, we went all over playing, and it was fantastic," she said.

Another player who, like Lyons, would have vividly remembered playing opposite Jeannie Allott was one of the lesser chronicled legends of the Scottish game. Inside right Edna Neillis – still a teenager, at the age of nineteen – set up the first goal in that first official England international.

She had grown up in the east end of Glasgow, a fervent supporter of Rangers, and while playing for a boys' side in the city caught the eye of the Celtic manager Jock Stein – who said if she had been a boy, he would have signed her.

She went on to play for Westthorn United, one of the teams who competed in the Butlin's Cup, a nationwide tournament for women's sides.

It was difficult for women to enjoy any degree of footballing success in Scotland. That was not to say there was no history of football in the country. In fact, the Scottish FA now proudly boasts that Hibernian Park in Edinburgh was the venue for the first known women's football match conducted under official rules, with a team from Scotland beating England 3–0 on 7th May 1881. Despite this – and despite Scotland finding similar take-up for women's football while the men's game was in abeyance during the first World War – the Scottish FA banned their members from advocating for the women's game. They took it a step further in 1948, banning the women's teams who had carried on their activities regardless from using any facilities and resources belonging to a member club, or from booking licensed match officials. In 1971, their country was the only one in Europe that had voted against taking women's football within the UEFA remit. It was at this point that the Scottish Women's FA was formed, in an effort to coordinate women's football in Scotland and to centralise their correspondence, negotiation and campaigning when it came to the Scottish FA. With all this going on, it was no wonder that a player as skilful as Neillis began to consider her options.

Elsie Cook, long-serving administrator of the Scottish Women's FA and manager of the Scotland women's team, helped Neillis put together a portfolio of her footballing achievements, which she took to a national paper in 1973. The *Daily Record* made the arrangements for her to play trials for Reims, in France, a country which had recognised women's football since 1968 and formally approved its existence in 1970. Though the French were impressed with her, a bigger club were soon alerted to her ability. Neillis signed for ACF Milan, winning the league and cup with them in 1975. Indeed, it was two goals from Neillis that sealed the victory in their final league match against Lazio.

In 1975, the *Sunday Post* ran a sizeable feature on the woman they called "a sun-tanned girl soccer star", who was back in Scotland on a break from her spell in Italy. They described her life there, with her home in "a luxurious, rent-free apartment" and meals "free daily nosh-ups in a restaurant". Neillis was coy about the money she was receiving, saying only that it was a "lot more than I earned when I was working in a factory". The article also underlined the contrast between Italy and Scotland when it came to women's football: "It's not the joke women's soccer is here." Neillis later moved to AFC Gorgonzola, where she won a third Italian Cup in 1980.

She returned to Scotland after the end of her playing career, which also included spells at Piacenza, Foggia and Lecce.

Yet Neillis was not alone on these adventures. Scotland team-mate Rose Reilly – also part of that inaugural official national team – was alongside her, then seventeen when she left the country, and it is Rose whose name has gone down in history, with her achievements feted. Eight years later, the *Sunday Post* ran a question-and-answer feature with Reilly (once again noting that "in Britain women's football is still treated as something of a joke"). She had no embarrassment about talking numbers, from the transfer fee of £20,000 that Lecce paid for her and the 6,000 fans who regularly attended home games, to the £700 a month she got in her monthly salary, and the £1,000 bonus the players each got if they won the league. These earnings were significantly more than the average for a woman aged over eighteen in the UK at the time; the average weekly wage than was around £98.90.

Reilly's football career began as a small child, when on the suggestion of a coach she cropped her hair short to play alongside the boys unobtrusively. Reilly's talent still made her stand out. In one match, she later recalled, she scored eight goals in front of a scout for her beloved Celtic. The scout approached the team's manager to ask if the amazingly talented number seven was available to sign. When he was told that the goal-scorer was a girl, he found it difficult to believe. Reilly was also incredulous that she could not sign for Celtic, even though she clearly stood out as gifted.

Unable to join Elsie Cook's Stewarton Thistle side until she was twelve, she counted down the days. Five years later, she joined Neillis on the move to Milan, reflecting in a later interview: "When the plane landed at Linate airport, the doors opened, the sun was out and it was like a mother's embrace. We played at the San Siro, in front of more than 20,000 people, and we won the league. For me there was never any question, I was staying in Italy."

Indeed, by 1984, Reilly had switched her footballing allegiance to Italy, making twenty-two appearances for them, and winning the prestigious invitational Mundialito, or "Little World Cup", with them in 1983 – as their captain. At league level, in total she won eight titles, with some incredible goal-scoring feats, including 45 goals in the 1980/81 season. In 1978/79, she even completed a spectacular double, winning the league in Italy with Lecce, playing their matches on a Saturday, and also with Reims, whose games were scheduled on Sundays. She also played for Milan, Catania, Trani, Napoli, Florence, Bari and Agliana, and spoke fluent Italian. Reilly's fame grew, with Lecce's sponsor using her in television commercials, and chat shows keen to book her as a guest. When she retired at the age of forty, she ran a sports shop in Sicily. She continued to play seven-a-side games for the local police team, and after tearing a calf muscle, was referred to a local doctor, Norberto Peralta, an Argentinian who had migrated to the island, and who became Reilly's husband. They had a daughter, Meghan, and the family stayed in Italy until 2001, when they moved to Scotland to care for Reilly's mother.

Neillis and Reilly were banned in 1975 – although, far from home, they knew nothing of the ban until Cook (also banned) sent them a letter to tell them. Reilly continues to claim she was puzzled by the decision, and got no clarity or reasoning behind it. It followed some outspoken media comments from several women involved in the game, criticising some choices made by the governing bodies, while others wondered if Neillis and Reilly had also blotted their respective copybooks for playing professionally, as so many of their English counterparts had been warned. (In fact, it remains unclear as to how this ban came into existence and even who made the decision; Dr Karen Fraser's PhD research says it was the Scottish Women's FA who banned Cook, while the Scottish FA themselves* say it was an SFA decision to ban all three of them "after calling for fairness and better support from the governing body".)

The sniping over rules and regulations even made it into the media coverage. The *Sunday Post* reported in May 1977 that, ahead of a clash with England, Scotland were without nine of their best players due to their moves to teams in Milan and Rome, explaining it thus: "The [Scottish FA] claim these girls are professionals, and as such are not allowed to play for Scotland, an all-amateur outfit. The [Scotland Women's Football Association] say they are still amateurs and are frantically trying to get the Italian FA to clarify the girls' status."

Indeed, as the article implies, Italy proved a successful second home for many Scottish players seeking a more professional set-up, from the 1970s onwards; June Hunter,

* https://150.scottishfa.co.uk/scottish-football-history/a-history-of-womens-football-in-scotland/

another who played in the 1972 match against England, also joined Gorgonzola, later moving to Giolli Gelati Roma, then Piacenza, marrying an Italian man and settling there. Sheila Begbie, who went on to become an integral part of Scotland's work to increase participation in women's football, was offered a move to Trani when Reilly was there, but ultimately decided to turn it down because of a competing job offer – as a PE teacher in Edinburgh.

In 1998, the Scottish FA finally took charge of the women's international set-up as well as development centres for girls. The Scottish Women's Premier League was launched in 2002, with a second division added in 2016, and Scotland reached their first ever major tournament finals a year later.

Reilly was inducted into the Scottish Football Hall of Fame in 2007. Twelve years later, the Scottish FA finally awarded caps as mementos to those women who played in the 1972 match against England.

Neillis died aged sixty-two in 2015. Alison Johnstone, Green Party member of the Scottish Parliament for Lothian, submitted a motion that described her as a "pioneer of Scottish sport", hailing her "highly successful spell" in Italy, and supporting "calls for Ms Neillis's legacy to be honoured by her induction into the Football Hall of Fame". Neillis was later recognised in this way, posthumously inducted in 2018.

"Edna knew she was good. She transcended the women's game at a time that females were still trying to get past that male domination. She simply took the ball and jinked it everywhere. She wasn't physical – Edna was mercurial. A will o' the wisp – passed you, wi' the ball, bouncing off all parts of her spare body. And a backward glint of triumph tossed back at yae. She defo toyed with all defences, took no prisoners... but her joyous love of football was a sight to see. The best of the best."

"Glasgow made Edna. She had the typical Glasgow sense of humour and never took herself too seriously. Made the best of everything and then turned it into a humorous story."

Those tributes came from a former opponent, Theresa Coffey of Dundee Strikers, and a former team-mate, Sheena McCulloch. Her friend Elsie Cook could talk at length about her memories of a great player and an exceptional human being, and would unsurprisingly find herself getting a little emotional about it at times.

They first met at the Butlin's Cup when her team Stewarton Thistle faced Neillis's Westthorn United. They walked out on to the pitch beside each other, and though many of the players were nervous, Neillis began singing 'Maggie May' at the top of her voice.

"This wee redhead started singing at the top of her voice! She was just daft on Rod Stewart. I just couldn't stop laughing, she was hilarious. We were alongside each other, walking on to the park, and then I just fell in love with her. She was such a character. She was such a kind, generous person, and so funny – she could have been a stand-up comedian, a Billy Connolly type. She had too much to say, and she had so much to say that made you laugh. It didn't matter what the occasion was, Edna was always just Edna."

Neillis grew up in Ruchazie, in Glasgow, and played football with the boys in the street. When she started work in a local factory (which Cook thought distilled whiskey), she would play with her colleagues.

"She didn't care about life in general, like money and having this and having that. She just cared about football and being nice."

Standing just five feet and two inches with "really skinny white legs", Cook likened her friend to the Celtic winger Jimmy Johnston, hugely technically gifted, and who simply enjoyed the challenge of beating players.

It was ironic that the most suitable comparison for Neillis's style of play was a Celtic legend, because she was a Rangers fan. When Cook was approached by Celtic manager Jock Stein to bring two teams of women to Parkhead to play an exhibition match ahead of a European Cup tie, Neillis had firm views on how she would celebrate with the supporters of Rangers' fierce rivals.

"We were standing in the tunnel – two teams standing in the tunnel with Jock Stein. He heard Margaret McAuley saying to Edna, 'What are you going to do if you score a goal at Parkhead? You're a Rangers fan!'

"And Edna said, 'I'm not going to do nothing!'

"Oh my, she scored a cracking goal. I remember it was bucketing down, monsoon rain, and already the terraces were packed with the Celtic fans. They were all up and roaring about how wonderful she was, and oh, it was amazing, she did an aeroplane run right round the park – arms akimbo, away she went, splash, splash, splash! The fans really appreciated it, and so did Jock Stein."

When she and Reilly went to Reims, Cook said, the fans took to them immediately and the coach built the team around them.

"Rose was strong, physically strong and fast, she was an athlete, but Edna was more just like the boy in the street that's got something special, she was just amazing, technically, so gifted. She was better than Rose, technically, but Rose was very, more determined and more athletic."

Cook was secretary of the Scottish Women's Football Association when Reilly and Neillis were banned, and she still said she did not understand the reasoning behind it.

"Look at it nowadays, at women's football. They play everywhere. They can go to whatever country they want to play in, and be accepted."

Unlike Reilly, Neillis found it difficult to settle in Italy, suffering from bouts of homesickness. "Her heart was never over there," said Cook, "her heart was in Scotland."

However, like Reilly, she had been asked to play for Italy. She refused.

"Edna did not want to play for Italy. Edna was Scottish. She told them, 'I'm Scottish. I'm not going to play for Italy.'"

Towards the end of her life, Neillis suffered from poor health, and had her legs amputated. Cook was unsure of the detail, but remembered the last time they met up, a gathering of former team-mates at Hampden Park.

"The girls came from all over Scotland just to meet Edna, because they knew what had happened to her, with her illness. She was the life and soul of the party that day. Everybody was laughing, everybody was happy.

"I sat beside her at one point in the afternoon, my mother with me as well – my mum just worshipped her, my girls worshipped her, everybody worshipped her, she was just that kind of person, she was so selfless and kind – and I was asking her, 'What happened [with your health]?' and she was away to tell me, still laughing, and somebody interrupted the conversation, so I never found out exactly what it was."

Just as their counterparts in England and Wales had done, the Scottish FA had made some kind of restitution towards the female internationals who had represented their country and had little recognition or reward. Reilly, Margaret McAuley, Linda Kidd and Jean Stewart received their souvenir caps in 2019, while others got them presented in December 2023 ahead of the current team's UEFA Women's Nations League match against England. It was, of course, too late for Neillis, whose former team-mate Liz Smith picked hers up on her behalf. Smith handed it on to Cook, who was donating it to Scottish football's Hall of Fame.

Cook had fought so hard for help from the establishment to run her teams, from councils to the Scottish FA itself, that the interest around the game's history now almost bewildered her: "Scotland were so straight-laced where it came to men and women. Women were at the kitchen sink. Men were out working and they were in charge. Oh, they were in charge of everything, absolutely everything.

"When I went into the council offices in Kilmarnock, I said to the lady, 'Can I book the Howard Park in Kilmarnock for a game on Sunday?' and she just looked at me: 'What's the name of the team?'

"I said, 'Stewarton Thistle Ladies.'

"'We don't agree with ladies playing football. The ladies cannae use the parks.'

"Goodness me. That was the early 1960s. So we used to slip onto the park and play and just go home manky. These girls were going home on two buses, three buses, to get back, because we were a small village, and it was all the wee villages around about the girls came from. It wasn't as if it was a big city with loads of people in; it was difficult finding players, but the lasses that did come along were fantastic.

"It was dreadful back then, and that's when we could have done with the reports in the paper and people standing up for us. We hadn't done anything wrong. All you wanted to do was to kick a ball."

She added: "So many good lassies have passed away, and there was just so much to tell. It seems to be the same folk like myself that are telling over and over again, 'These girls were amazing, amazing players.'"

This was certainly the case with Neillis. Her mother and siblings had long since passed away, so it was difficult to fill in some of the blanks about her early life, leaving it up to her former team-mates to tell her story as best they could.

⚽

When Janice Lyons looked back over half a century and was asked if she had any regrets about the choices she made, she said she had none.

"Not really. I do regret not playing for England and not getting picked. But I've no regrets about going to Italy. It was one of the best things I've done in my life as a young footballer, because you've got to live your dream.

"The opportunities are there now for people to do what they want to, – it's not frowned upon now, is it? It certainly was frowned upon then, because they'd say, 'You're leaving your job to go play there? You must be mad!

"And they didn't realise the dream that I had. It was an ambition. I've got to do it."

Lyons' pragmatism is remarkable – even more so in the context of her departure from Italy two years later. Her mother had been experiencing poor health, which was a factor in her decision to return home, but she also thought she ought to think about her future and her income. She got a job with Manchester City Council, and though she wanted to go back to Corinthians, many of her friends had moved on.

"All the great players, they had left or moved on, got married, or different lives," she said, "and I went back, but it was never the same. The team, when we were playing for Manchester Corinthians at the time I did, it was so good. It was excellent. We was winning everywhere. We had a major reputation and we still have, but the time I went back, they was dying on their feet really, and they were getting players in that weren't good enough. And so no, I didn't, I didn't play for them anymore. I stopped that."

Of course, at the time, it was not as simple a decision as a modern professional might take – calling their agent to find a new club – or even a top amateur, using her network of contacts to find somewhere that might be a good fit for her, her talents and her requirements. There were not many women's clubs in the country, let alone in the area. Lyons could have gone to old rivals Fodens as they were not too far away from her home in Handforth, in Sandbach, but she felt that there were some lines that just could not be crossed. She also thought that Fodens were suffering from a similar issue to Corinthians, with some of their great players now moving on and not being replaced adequately.

So Janice Lyons – shortly after returning from her successful spell in Italy – hung up her boots for good.

"I didn't play. I wish I [had] done, looking back, but I didn't find the right team.

"But there were no other teams then. There was nothing really, like it is now, you can play for a local team. You had to travel to a team then. That's a regret, that I didn't come back and play, because I was only early twenties. I had enough time to do it. But you meet other people in your life, you like to go out and you're not committed as much – I'll hold my hands up, I probably wasn't. But thinking back, because you can think of things in hindsight, yes, I wish I had [carried on playing].

"But I didn't."

LEARNER

It is perhaps a little ironic that despite UEFA members passing a vote in 1971 to permit women's football, the governing bodies of both the countries that Sue Lopez knew well failed to integrate their women's game properly until much later: Italy in 1986, England in 1993. Yet their experiences were in direct contrast to one another. The Women's FA soldiered on in England, at least recognised by the FA as the "sole governing body of women's football" across the country, but wary of the double-edged sword of publicity and particularly nervous of anything that might be judged to be commercialism, while the smart businesspeople in Italy continued to run their successful league and continued to attract foreign players over there, lured not just by the expenses covered but by the prospect of genuine competition.

Lopez reports that England captain Debbie Bampton chose to play for Trani in Italy because there was not a genuine national league available in England, just regional ones, and when she arrived there she discovered that club football there was far ahead of anything she had experienced.

When Bampton signed for Trani in 1987, she played alongside a compatriot there, Kerry Davis, with whom she had played in the final of the 1984 inaugural Women's European

Championships. She had also captained her in the England squad that went to Italy in 1985 for the Mundialito tournament, an invitational forerunner to the Women's World Cup. Martin Reagan's side lifted the trophy, finishing second in the group stage with a win, a draw and a loss, and then beating Italy 3-2 in the final. Davis scored a goal in the second group match, a 1–1 draw against Italy in the Stadio Giovanni Chiggiato, Caorle, and evidently the striker's performances caught the eye.

When Davis returned home, she got a phone call from Anne O'Brien. O'Brien, an Ireland international, had joined Stade de Reims in 1973, and moved on to Italy after that. She was with Lazio in 1985, a club she would later coach, and she was tasked with asking Davis if she would be interested in joining.

Davis was not the only England player that Lazio were interested in; they also liked the look of midfielder Marieanne Spacey. The pair of them flew out to have a look around, and though Spacey opted to return to England, Davis decided to stay. She was working in a sports centre and living with her parents back at home, and for her it was the easiest of choices to play football full-time instead. The club arranged for her to stay in a room with the mother-in-law of one of the directors, and she also enrolled in school to learn Italian.

"I didn't know any words when I got there, but the classes that I went to were for people who already spoke Italian!" she said. "So it was an absolute struggle, honestly, my goodness. Even when Maura [Furlotti], who was the captain of Lazio at the time, used to help me with my homework, she said,

'My goodness, Kerry, even for me, Italian-speaking, this is tough, this is tough!'"

Davis was lucky that she had team-mates that spoke reasonable English, even though Anne O'Brien left the club a few months after her arrival. Despite her best efforts, her Italian remained limited, but she decided to stay in the country anyway: "I'll tell you what, it wasn't easy. Wasn't easy."

That was not just a linguistic issue. She found the slower pace of life in Italy very tricky to cope with, but also found it difficult to fill her time in Rome, not being able to access English media very easily.

"People rave about Rome, but it's very small. If you're a tourist, you could probably do it in a couple of days, most of the touristy spots, but I liked it. My team-mates were very friendly, very helpful, really good people, good people to be around. So I did like Rome. I was just probably a bit bored because I couldn't interact as much as I wanted to. And in Rome also, all the girls were at work during the day, so I spent a lot of time on my own."

It was quite a lonely time in places. She considered returning to England for good after the end of her first season with Lazio – and indeed did go back home – until she got an offer from Trani, on the south-eastern coast. The lure was too much; Davis liked the fact that Italy had a national league and better organisation than she was used to in England, where the domestic competition was still organised regionally and tended to be dominated by two or three teams.

Davis signed up for private Italian lessons with a tutor,

and found herself making progress on her new timetable. Trani trained most days, and ran their sessions during the day, whereas Lazio had trained in the evening.

"Half the team were based in Trani, but we had players that used to travel from Milan, so they'd jump on a train Friday night, sleep on the train – they'd have the sleeper trains – and then they would play Saturday afternoon. The kick-off times varied depending on the time of the year, so they were mostly two o'clock kick-off, three o'clock kick-off, but as it got hotter, then they put the kick-off back.

"We had an athletic coach and the manager-cum-coach. There was a little stadium in Trani, and the women's team was better than the men's, so it was quite successful over the years. [Trani] was much, much better [than Rome] but still, they relax a lot. They had the siesta and things like that. I wasn't used to that. I needed to be doing something."

Trani had two apartments for their players, one by the sea, which was essentially the squad's social hub, and one further inland, which was more to Davis's taste.

She was a central part of England's squad at the time, but even with her goal-scoring record, playing international matches was not easy. She paid for her own flights to get back for England camp: "If I hadn't have done that, I wouldn't have been playing for England in the 1980s, trust me." With the benefit of decades of distance, she was also prepared to confess to some rule-breaking; the Women's FA, still in control of the England set-up at the time, had a rule where players were not allowed to take part in a match within the seven days ahead of an international, which was difficult for Davis, as of course the Italian league was not structured around when the Women's FA scheduled matches for England.

"I can say now that I used to break the rules all the time. I used to play before an England game. I remember one time a game at Reading. I flew in late, the flight was delayed, and when I got to the hotel everyone had gone to bed. I was rooming with [goalkeeper] Terry Wiseman, and she waited up for me, and we kept it quiet that I'd got in so late."

The record books suggest that this match was the 4–0 win against the Republic of Ireland on 27th April 1986. Davis scored twice, en route to a then-record England goals tally of 44. She was confident that manager Martin Reagan had no issue with her making her own decisions about her footballing career, but remembered a Women's FA officer telling her that if she could not make both matches scheduled in a short period, then she would not be selected ever again.

"I'm surprised women's football got to where it is," she said. "I'm pretty sure Martin wouldn't have been so ruthless. [I thought,] 'You forget, mate, that I pay for my own flights to come back to play for England.' If I hadn't have, I wouldn't have got my 82 England caps for sure."

Davis stayed in Italy until 1989, spending a season with Napoli after her two campaigns with Trani, returning to England at the age of twenty-seven and rejoining Crewe Alexandra. The local newspaper hailed her return, describing her as a "soccer star" when they reported her call-up to the England squad in September 1989. Although she had enjoyed her time in Italy, she had not made money, and she had no savings cushion for the future, so, as she put it, she "had to come back and go to the real world". She went on to play for Knowsley (later Liverpool), and Croydon, and was part of the first England squad to play in a Women's World Cup, in 1995.

In an era before the popularisation of mobile phones and social media, it was difficult to keep in touch with old team-mates from Italy, or to visit them as regularly as she would have liked. However, she had continued with her Italian lessons. Unsurprisingly, when she first returned to England, her language learning was less of a priority, but she had found local universities offering reasonably priced courses.

"I speak OK, I understand OK, but I struggle with the grammar!" she admitted.

She had also found herself in a media spotlight she never expected, hailed as the first woman of colour to play for England, inducted into the National Football Museum's Hall of Fame, and interviewed on television for Black History Month. Proud of her heritage, with her father born in the Caribbean, she realised the significance of her achievements long after she hung up her boots.

"I'll take anything that comes my way," she said, "because it's for my generation, and the generation before me."

Sian Williams headed to Italy after she finished school. A technical, gifted, classy midfielder, she had applied for university, but football dominated her life, and she had seen a television programme featuring both Kerry Davis and Rose Reilly which inspired her to consider the possibility of playing in Italy. The documentary, called *Home and Away*, aired on BBC One on 7th January 1987, with the *Evening Telegraph* describing Davis and Reilly as "the female equivalents of [England striker] Mark Hateley and [Scotland midfielder] Liam Brady, even if their pay packets don't quite match up".

"You never used to see women's football at all back in the day," she recalled. "All of a sudden, I thought, 'There's somewhere out there I can play.'

"It was really lucky I got over there. There were no contacts, no agents or things like that. I was playing for Millwall at the time. We went to Milan to play a tournament. From the tournament, a couple of the teams asked me to go and sign. In those days there was no connections, no links, it was a bit of luck as much as anything that I made a contact, so I had the choice of going to AC Milan or the team that I went to; I chose to go to Juve Siderno."

It was almost as straightforward as she made it sound. From playing in the tournament one weekend, she had signed and was in Juve Siderno's starting line-up within the week. Essentially, she had three days to pack up her life.

"That's what I wanted to do. I didn't even think twice. My mum was in tears as I left! They were very supportive. My mum didn't come over with me, but my dad said, 'You don't know these people, I'm coming over with you.' He flew over with me, stayed a couple of days. We actually flew into

Naples because we were due to play away that day, and he stayed for a few days and he just decided, yeah, it was OK, they were nice. He was like, 'Stay with these people, these [people] will look after you.'"

Williams's parents were supportive of her football, although her mother may have harboured tentative dreams that one day she might give it up and select a couple of more traditionally feminine hobbies. Her father in particular encouraged her to chase her dreams, however distant they may seem. He knew from his own experiences that working hard would get you a long way; Alan Williams MP was the son of a miner who moved into civil service. He did well at school, progressing to study for a degree, and later becoming an economics lecturer before moving into journalism, and then winning the seat of Swansea West in 1964. He was in parliament for the best part of half a century.

"My dad was [from] Cardiff, Splott, and my mum was from the Tredegar Valley. My dad grew up in quite poor circumstances, his dad was a coal miner, his grandad was a coal miner. He would have been brought up from an early age: 'Work really hard to get out so you don't have to go down the mine.' So he always instilled that in us – work hard whatever it is. That's what I think about football. Whatever you do, you work really hard to do it. Obviously I wasn't quite as academically motivated as him, but [with] football I was, so he backed me on that."

Contrary to the claims made by some internet databases, Williams was born in Bexleyheath, and had spent all her life in South London. She was fortunate to be in that area when Millwall Lionesses launched their girls' teams, and she stepped up to senior football at the age of thirteen. She had competed for her primary school team, although never playing against another girl.

"Every week you'd hear, 'Oh, look, they've got a girl,' and I think that's what made me quite quiet and shy, because you felt like you were always being looked at. One or two teams did kick up a fuss, but in fairness my PE teacher there was like, 'She can play, she's playing, and that's it.'"

Williams had a brother two years older than her, so was used to playing alongside and opposite bigger boys, which pushed her to get better.

"I think it also helped me keep my feet on the ground," she mused. "Sometimes you see players nowadays and they're heralded as this, that and the other, but because you were always playing against boys two years older, you never thought you were particularly good. Some of the boys used to go, 'You know you're good?' I used to be like, 'Yeah, not better than you!'"

Williams was ushered into the international set-up courtesy of her Millwall Lionesses team-mate Jane Bartley, who played for Wales, and asked the coaches whether she could bring her young colleague to a training camp. They agreed, inviting her over to the Isle of Man for training and then a friendly match, in which she was named in the starting line-up.

"It was a really good experience, but it was a bit of a whirlwind, I didn't know too much about it. Then I went to a couple of training camps after that, but my dad had to pay for my camp because [the Wales set-up] didn't have the money. They said, 'We can get you a [souvenir] cap, but you have to pay' – I didn't know at the time, but my dad told me many years later, he said he wanted me to have it. You had to pay for your own hotel, a thousand in a room to keep the cost low. It was pretty amateurish, but at the end of the day people were at least trying to make things happen. They did it within the constraints of no one supporting, no one was interested, nobody wanted to back women's football – women's sport, even."

When Williams announced her intentions to go to Italy, she was told that if she did, she would never again be selected for Wales. She was confused initially, and explained that, if it was a financial issue, her club would be happy to pay for her flights back. However, that was not the problem: it was a rule being laid down, and one that still puzzled her.

"Why would you want to hold a player back? It didn't make any sense to me."

With her rent and her food all paid for by her club in Italy, the threat of ending her international recognition from Wales made no difference to Williams's plans. The Juve Siderno players were spread across three apartments in the city, with a cook preparing their meals for them, and a small stipend for any additional expenses they had. As an eighteen-year-old, Williams needed nothing else.

Yet she was soon aware that, although she could have easily stayed out there and lived like that for years, it was not enough to build a life on; there was no way to accrue savings, and she knew that, should her footballing career end prematurely, she had little to prepare her for another line of work. She considered studying for a degree in Italy, but the paperwork proved problematic, which in hindsight she thought was for the best as tertiary education in a second language might have proved too difficult. Instead, she returned to England, and signed up for a maths degree at Loughborough University, one of the best regarded sporting institutions in the country.

Her first year at university were what she described as a "culture shock": not because she was out of practice when it came to study, but because she had gone from a high standard of football in Italy to a much lower level in England. She travelled back and forward from the Midlands to Millwall, but eventually only bothered making the journey a couple of times a season, for the most competitive league matches. In her second year, however, she was allowed to train with the men's university team, which meant she got practice at a better standard of play. By the end of her time at university, she signed for Arsenal, and the FA had launched the National League, with the intent of improving the competition, operating domestically and with the best teams in the country playing against each other, rather than playing in a regional league. Williams was curious to see what happened, and did not go back to Italy.

"I found it frustrating," Williams said of the domestic league that Millwall were competing in. "I thought the university standard was better. I suppose looking back with hindsight, it's logical that at that time it wouldn't have been high. I felt you'd come from this high quality competitive league [in Italy] to this.

"Then I went and joined Arsenal because Millwall had actually changed managers and he didn't play a style of football that I was ever going to get in. He was very much about winning the ball, getting it forward early, being strong, and I thought, 'Well, I can see the writing on the wall here!'"

She also did not return to the Wales set-up. The under-21s had a match against England for which Williams would have been eligible, and she was not selected. Knowing that she had been told that she would not play for Wales again, England selected her to play for them instead, but Wales objected. It took three years and a lot of paperwork between Wales, England, the FA, UEFA and Arsenal to untangle this particular mess.

"I was basically a child that turned up to something, I played in a friendly, and then they're saying I can't play international football," she reflected. A new rule was devised permitting players to represent a different country if they had initially played under the age of eighteen outside of formal tournaments. Williams was allowed to play for England, just as Jeannie Allott went on to play for the Netherlands, and Rose Reilly for Italy.

"It's astounding, but I suppose back in the day there was no real structure, there were no real rules. Women had only just been allowed to start playing, so they hadn't really thought it through.

"It was very different. If you spoke up at the time you were a troublemaker. Oh, OK, just standing up for a little bit of equality, that makes you a troublemaker?"

With Williams integral to the side, Arsenal became one of the dominant forces in the new National League, along with Doncaster Belles and, briefly around the millennium, Fulham, who offered their players full-time professional contracts in a blaze of publicity. The increased standard of play and competition was enough to keep Williams interested.

"We [at Arsenal] had lots of players that were really driven over the years, Vic [Akers, the manager] was really driven, and then we also had a big name [of Arsenal] behind us. Doncaster, they were very successful, there were teams that were very successful, but I think having the name as well, the combination drove women's football forward. We dragged women's football kicking and screaming into a professional attitude, where there were a lot of teams that got away with just talent and then [saw]: 'Oh, well, Arsenal are working harder than us, we need to work harder!' Having the name of Arsenal got the media a little bit more interested, so it made a big difference."

Reflecting on her decision to stay with Arsenal rather than consider moving elsewhere or going abroad again, she added: "There was always something where you thought, 'I'll stay another year, I'll stay another year, I'll stay another year,' and you suddenly realise, 'I haven't gone anywhere else, I haven't done anything else.' It was good; like, you could see how the game had developed over that period of time. By the time I finished playing we had a team that would compete in [today's full-time, fully-professional top flight] WSL [Women's Super League], obviously if we were full-time and training. Still, you'd have to travel long distances and win 7 or 8–0, and that was tedious. That in the end was what ground me down. I don't really want to travel five or six hours to go and beat someone 5 or 6–0."

After completing her degree, she went on to qualify as a teacher, although she decided to leave Loughborough and study elsewhere: "I thought, 'If I [go] to Loughborough I won't get any work done because all my friends are there!' I wasn't the most studious student, I have to be honest with you. I went to Bedford, it's De Montfort [University] now. I thought, 'I don't know anyone there, I might be able to do some work,' and it was closer to Arsenal, obviously I could come down and train, I could train all the time."

She taught for a few years in conjunction with her playing commitments, and then took a role within Arsenal's academy, allowing her more access to footballing facilities while also earning a wage, rather than being forced to take unpaid leave from school whenever she needed to travel, particularly after the launch of the Europe-wide competition of the UEFA Women's Cup, later the Women's Champions League. This was at the time that Fulham were investing in their women's team, and Arsenal knew they needed to keep up with them; having their players on site, whether they were in the academy, the community department or the training ground laundry, permitted more flexibility than a standard job. Williams and team-mates Jayne Ludlow and Emma Byrne all worked at the Arsenal academy and were able to go and play matches whenever required. However, domestically, the National League still was not as competitive as Williams would have wanted it.

"You want to have a challenge. You go out and play Liverpool, you play Doncaster, you know you're going to have a challenge. Everyone's different; some people like winning 5–0. For me, that wasn't what really excited me."

She did, however, have one last hurrah, playing in the USA for three months. It was an option she had had earlier in her career, when she considered entering the collegiate system on a sports scholarship, but she decided against it. Then in the summer of 2005, Emma Hayes – one of Arsenal's academy players prior to a career-ending injury – was coaching in the USA, and told Williams that New York Magic were looking for a midfielder.

"There was myself and a Japanese player sharing this apartment. It was only small, but we were a five-minute walk from the Empire State Building. We spent a summer out there. So that was a really good experience.

"I just thought, 'Let's do something while there's an opportunity.'"

Williams's England career stretched across seventeen years; and to any onlooker, her tally of twenty caps would seem far too few. However, the numbers make more sense when one considers that she played two matches for England under the auspices of the Women's FA and coach John Bilton before the responsibility was transferred to the FA and coach Ted Copeland. In the two decades that the Women's FA ran a representative England team, they played just 113 matches. Even in 1993/94, the first season under FA control, they played only six matches. Added to the simple lack of matches that Williams could have played in was another, more fundamental issue: a contrast in footballing outlooks between her and coach Copeland. She pointed to the England campaign at the 1995 Women's World Cup as an example of where their footballing principles clashed. Indeed, Williams herself was an unused substitute for all four of England's matches in Sweden, and was also not keen on the way players were treated.

"We went to Sweden, we were there for three weeks and they were like, 'Oh, you can't go out of the hotel.' What do you think's going to happen to us? We're in Sweden! It's not like we're in a war zone. 'No, you can't go out.'

"We're grown adults! I can understand it if you had a sixteen-year-old in your squad, you might want to be a bit more careful, but we were grown adults. I said, 'You know, I take kids on school trips. I can cope with walking around a city on my own.'"

After hanging up her boots, Williams returned to teaching in combination with coaching, most notably as head coach of Wales. It was no surprise that the way she approached that role was shaped by her experiences with England.

"You're an adult, you make a decision. You stay up till two o'clock in the morning and you play crap, that's your problem, but you're an adult, you make a decision. I recommend this [behaviour], but I'm not going to tell you [that] you should get up early or shouldn't go to bed late. Why would you do that? Why would you treat people like it's a school trip?"

She followed those three years with a spell as Watford's head coach. However, neither part-time role paid the bills, and she knew she would have to make a sensible decision to ensure a financially safe future.

"My life up to then had revolved around football. I had to have that element of common sense. I had no pension, I had no real security in that respect. I had bought my house, but I was struggling to pay for that, and when the financial crisis hit, I had no choice, I could carry on with Watford or I could go full-time at work at school. I tried doing both but it just killed me, so in the end I had to say, 'I can't carry on with it,' which was a shame, in a way, but I probably would have been in hospital sick by the end of the year if I'd carried on trying to do both.

"I couldn't really afford to keep going with it, to be honest with you."

As a teacher, Williams became involved with the Hertfordshire county representative teams, and from there the national English Schools squads, taking up the position of head coach for the girls under-15s.

"I just suddenly thought, 'I could help here, I could give the girls something here,' because I've got a lot of experience, it seems silly to waste it. These are kids with ambition, kids with talent, and anything I can pass on, that might help them, so when the role came up I applied for it."

It was a role Williams really enjoyed because of the pleasing balance between achievement and enjoyment.

"It's not too regimented. It's all about, yes, high performance but because it's schools-based, it's always the person comes first, and that's good. For some of those girls, they'll never play for England again. You just don't know. That's just the harsh reality of junior football, and you want it to be something they can take away with them for the rest of their life, look back on and think, 'Yeah, that was brilliant,' and those that do go on and play [at a higher level], it's a stepping stone in the learning process for them. I think sometimes there's a tendency for junior coaches to get too carried away. Rome wasn't built in a day. This is a long process, just chill out. It's a long process, little snippets of information, bit by bit."

Many business-focused studies had suggested that senior female leaders had often benefited from playing team sports in their childhood, and Williams felt strongly that the qualities her players developed – such as resilience and determination – would serve them well in their future careers in whatever field. She also worked with the boys' academy at Stevenage Borough, and liked their mantra of "better people, better players", saying that it showed their awareness that even in men's football only a very few would ever make it to the top, and that clubs had a responsibility to care for their young players regardless of the path they chose to follow.

It was a fine coaching career that very nearly foundered at its very beginning. Williams had taken her first coaching badge while at university, and as an England player was later invited on to a women-only B Licence course. However, she did not complete it then, and on deciding to go back to it a few years later, she once again found herself in a bureaucratic struggle; the Welsh FA could not find the records of her first coaching badge, and the English FA would not allow her to take the B Licence without it. Although frustrated ("I threw my toys out of the pram," she admitted), she eventually opted to go through the entire process again.

That was not to say that these courses were easy or even straightforward, particularly in terms of their dynamic and their atmosphere. She recalled one session she went to while still a young player, which had only one other female coach in attendance, and some of the male delegates were less than welcoming to what they perceived as young women invading their space.

"There were times when it was difficult, the old days, the courses were very much testosterone-run. I suppose at the time nobody meant anything by it but it was very much the male jokes and sometimes you felt a little bit awkward, so you had to grow a thick skin."

She wondered whether the men felt behaving in such a fashion was simply an expectation at the time.

"You'd have to say they're probably not bad people, but that was the way it was and nobody would stop to think they're being really unpleasant or stopped to think about it. Certainly in football, some people felt, 'What are women doing in our game?' Without question there was an element of that."

It made Williams all the more determined to ensure that other women coming into the environment were not as isolated. She felt confident within herself and her abilities because she knew she was a good footballer, but understood that other women might not feel so secure in the situation.

"If there's another female on the course I try and make contact," she said. "I'll go and sit with them because I know how I felt – we're still very much in a minority."

Williams was also very wary of clubs and owners who would engage coaches and not pay them, especially in the women's professional game.

"Even now they want you to do something for nothing. I played for nothing my whole career apart from Italy, and a bit of semi-pro money towards the end... but you can't expect my generation to also coach for nothing.

"Now I dig my heels in about it. There are some men who will [coach in women's football] for nothing because they're trying to build their career, knowing that they can go into men's football.

"That's our game. You're making it so that we can't get paid because you are willing to do it for nothing."

Williams rarely spoke about her footballing career to the children she taught or coached unless she was asked directly.

"It's difficult, because a lot of people see it as a big deal, whereas you just think, 'That's my life, it's just an opportunity I had, so I pursued it,' but with the kids at school, when they ask, I'll go through it because they need to understand women didn't always have the opportunities and actually it's still not equal."

Many of the teenage girls she worked with did not see themselves facing any inequalities, and she warned them that they may find themselves facing discrimination at some point. It was important, she thought, to acknowledge and learn from history, which she really wanted to see within women's football as well: "It's important that players understand there's a history, where it's come from, where it needs to go still as well."

The nuances of each country's history were also important to acknowledge; while England might be making progress, other leagues and teams had fallen behind them.

"Every country's story is going to be different," she said. "When I was in Italy, my captain and one or two players, they used to come back [from international duty] with bags of kit; every time they represented their country they got a solid gold coin, and they used to come back with DVD players, they were given all this stuff. We had to pay for caps! It was hilarious.

"Every country was at a slightly different stage. It's quite interesting when you look at it and see Italy went into a lull and didn't progress after being the top league in the world for a while, they just seemed to plateau, whereas now they're putting money into it, lots of big clubs in [the domestic league] as well. Hopefully they'll progress again because they've got such a rich history in the game. But everyone is leapfrogging each other. At the moment, we're top dogs, and Wales and Scotland and Ireland, their players are benefiting because they're getting the opportunities to play full-time in the WSL.

"So for British football and Irish football, it's a positive time: you just have to stay in front of other people."

MASTER

"Teams were going abroad and playing in front of thousands of people back in the day!" said Elaine McHardy. "But the trouble is, there were no internet, no this, no that, a lot of things were not put down."

As a child growing up just outside Manchester, McHardy had played football with the boys before joining a local factory team that eventually became subsumed into Ashton United and became their official women's team. She and her friends went to watch them before they began playing for them, and recalled two heavy defeats to the two heavyweights of women's football in Manchester – 40–0 to Fodens, 19–0 to Corinthians, as far as McHardy's memory could establish. Within a few years, though, McHardy and her team improved, later beating the mighty Fodens themselves 5–2.

As she got to know them, McHardy occasionally travelled with Fodens on their annual overseas tours, including their first trip to the Netherlands – the visit that gave Jeannie Allott the opportunity to move abroad. They saw Allott again when she returned to the north-west for her twenty-first birthday party, thrown by her father, and then unexpectedly on the touchline of another overseas match.

"She did come to see us one year when we were playing in

Belgium! She drove over, her and Coby, and they drove over to come and watch us in one of the matches."

McHardy had played alongside and against plenty of other internationals, and one of her best team-mates was Vanessa O'Brien.

"She was an all-round sports player, Vanessa, I think she played netball, hockey. She met one of our players, who got talking to Nessa about football, and she came and had a look and then ended up signing for us.

"And what a player! Unbelievable player. Unbelievable at everything she did."

When Vanessa O'Brien arrived at Kingsley Westside FC, in the north of Perth, Australia, they had no female players at the club at all.

Within three years of her taking up her voluntary role there, they had girls' teams at under-8s, under-10s, under-12s, under-14s and under-16s, totalling around 150 young players.

'Soccer' has historically not been an Australian sport, taking a back seat to Aussie Rules football, cricket and rugby. That lack of sporting tradition compounded the struggles women in Australia faced if they wanted to play football. The Australian Women's Soccer association was founded in 1974. Much like the murky and confusing beginnings of women's international football in England, there were teams who were referred to as 'Australia' and competing at invitational events, but were not officially endorsed by the governing body. Some of those early achievements were finally recognised in 2023, but for decades the first official Australian national team was considered to be the ones who played New Zealand in New South Wales in October 1979. (The fact that this was an official team does not, however, mean they were provided with many resources: they were so pressed for money that they were unable to travel or host many other teams, with their next seven formal matches all against the same opponent, their near neighbours.)

By 2023, Football Australia boasted that 190,746 women and girls were involved in the game across the country, roughly 50,000 more than had been registered five years previously. In 1983, there had been just over 7,000 women playing, and 21,000 in 1997. As she reflected on her club's progress in the summer of 2024, O'Brien was hopeful that, by the time the next season started, there would be two senior women's teams as well, with players at other clubs looking to move due to their dissatisfaction at the way they were being treated.

One of her pet projects was the development of walking football at the club, having met up with friends back in Manchester who had already started it. While some who were experienced eleven-a-side footballers found the pace and limitations of walking football difficult to adjust to, O'Brien found it straightforward.

"It's just discipline. If you're disciplined, you can do it."

O'Brien was notable for still getting minutes for her eleven-a-side team despite approaching her sixtieth birthday ("If needed, I will play. I love it. I'll still run around on there"), but it was questionable whether any of the people who were aware of her ability or her contribution to the running of the club also knew that she had her name in the record books for another reason – she was the first official goal-scorer for Wales's national women's team.

Wales's first international women's team played in 1973, against Ireland, but that 3–2 defeat in front of a reported 3,500 spectators was not within the auspices of the FAW, the country's governing body. It took two decades and some dedicated lobbying from players Michele Adams, Karen Jones and Laura McAllister to get the FAW on board, led by the supportive Alun Evans, then the FAW's general secretary.

It was in September 1993 that the first official Wales team took to the field, facing Iceland at Afan Lido and losing 1–0. It took a few more days until Wales scored their first goal – in their first competitive match in qualifying for the European Championships in Cwmbran.

With Wales two goals down in 32 minutes, Vanessa O'Brien scored ten minutes before the break to write her name in history.

"We had to go for many, many trials down at Bristol," she recalled, having lived in the north-west of England for her entire life, and having discovered she could be eligible to play for Wales almost by accident, responding to an advert for players. (Indeed, the local newspapers reported that she had "no connection at all with the country"; O'Brien herself was unsure of what her qualification ultimately was, while Elaine McHardy thought it was a Welsh great-grandparent.) "I was carrying an injury. I remember I had... I don't know what the hell it was, it was something with my foot."

Fortunately she did not have to drive herself – her husband Todd did that, and had been supportive of her football right from the start. When she got the call-up for Wales's first official match, she and the other players stayed in a hotel, with accommodation paid for, although they did not get any payment themselves. Indeed, in the information sheets distributed to players confirming their call-ups later in the season, the note from Mr Evans, the FAW's chief executive, observed: "Unfortunately, I have to advise you that the Association has overspent its budget for Women's International Football for the season 1993/94. Therefore, funding is not available for this match and a £10.00 fee will be charged towards the costs of hosting the match." (O'Brien could not remember if she had been asked for any money, but admitted: "I am sure if we were asked to we would have paid it to play.")

Their kits, however, left a little to be desired – they were designed for men and were unsurprisingly huge on the female players.

O'Brien's match shirt was now framed and hanging on her wall. She gestured at it.

"Look at the size there, 42-inch chest. Have I got a 42-inch chest?!"

She did not. In the days when even international matchday programmes included female players' height and weight, O'Brien was listed as standing at five feet four inches tall, and weighing seven stone and seven pounds.

She remembered the goal that she scored in that first match; once, she had had it on video, but had not seen it for years.

"It just came back out on the rebound, and then it fell to my feet and I just tapped it in. I couldn't believe it. I was like that," she opened her mouth and eyes wide, to indicate disbelief. "Just screaming."

O'Brien started playing football as a very small child, one of thirteen siblings, and part of her brothers' kickarounds in the alley behind their house. She played at primary school, and went to the trials for the school's representative team. She was selected, but then was not allowed to play; other schools would not compete against a side including a girl. After that, her brothers set up a team, and O'Brien joined in with them – when they would let her: "I was a better player than them so they wouldn't pick me sometimes!"

O'Brien's footballing career took a diversion when she met up with an old school friend who remembered her skill and invited her to come along to a training session with a team in Ashton. As soon as O'Brien took to the field, they asked her to sign permanently.

"That was Ashton United," she said. "But it was the usual – you just used to get changed on the side of the park, no changing rooms.

"We used to get hammered, 20–0, 30–0, but then we started getting a few younger players and then we started building up a team."

Ashton United became Ladyblues, later winning the All-England five-a-side competition and beating the likes of the mighty Arsenal along the way, and then Manchester Belle Vue. There was some local media interest in the woman who had scored dozens of goals for her club, with the *Rochdale Observer*, perhaps inevitably, referring to O'Brien as "belle of the ball" after her first Wales call-up.

She also later represented Leasowe Pacific, who became Everton, and Manchester United, in the years before the women's team was fully integrated into the parent club.

"They weren't interested one bit," she said. "The girls just used to scratch around for kit and stuff, but no, they didn't want to know."

Still, she had one moment in the spotlight when at Manchester United; she was working for Norweb, the electricity supplier for the north-west, who sponsored a hospitality box at Old Trafford, and she was invited to feature in a photo shoot with fellow Wales internationals from the men's team, Ryan Giggs and Mark Hughes. For some reason, the men were late withdrawals, leaving O'Brien on the pitch by herself and in her element – "pretending to head a ball, pretending to score a goal!"

Elaine McHardy had taken on voluntary roles in running clubs and eventually the local leagues and associations, and knew very well from her own experience how uninterested men's teams and indeed the wider community could be when it came to women's football. Ashton United changed their name to Ladyblues as a condition of sponsorship, which secured them kits, tracksuits and bags, among other things – well worth it, in the players' eyes. These deals were rare. McHardy spent years as secretary of the Manchester and Merseyside League, dealing with all the paperwork by hand, and investing in an electric typewriter to make her job a little easier ("I hated typing at school as well!"). She stopped playing due to a bad knee injury at a time when the surgery to fix it would involve a seriously large incision and a lengthy recuperation time, and her role as secretary kept her involved. She even took the refereeing qualification ("I was the only woman when I went and did it at Manchester FA").

As has often been the case in women's football, after several changes of name and allegiance, McHardy's team – by then Manchester Belle Vue – split when the league restructured, and players had the chance to play locally but at a higher level of football. The players stayed in touch, though, and there were occasional reunions; McHardy recalled one memorable gathering for former Fodens players.

She admired the voluntary work O'Brien continued to do in Australia, to ensure the next generations of girls could play football, and highlighted that they and all women had always had to do extra work in their spare time just for the right to kick a ball.

"Starting off at Ashton United, for the privilege of playing on the pitch, we had to clean the men's dressing rooms twice a week when they trained. They didn't let us train on there. We used to train on a sports pitch, not far from there. So we had to go in, on a Tuesday and Thursday, when the men trained, afterwards, and clean the dressing rooms out, and help out with the tea on matchdays as well."

⚽

O'Brien and her family moved to Australia in 2005 to pursue a work opportunity for her husband. She picked up her involvement in football almost as soon as the plane touched down, coaching and playing. The organisation and dynamic of women's football in the new country was familiar to her – a certain lack of interest from men's clubs and the media, less solid infrastructure in place, fewer resources.

"It's just – yeah. Not good with women's football," she explained.

She was intending to carry on playing eleven-a-side football for as long as possible; the new "Masters league" that had been set up to cater for over-35s was of no interest to her, because it had a rule allowing three players younger than the age category per team.

One of O'Brien's close friends in Australia had a fascinating football tale of her own. Ann Gourley had been thinking about emigrating from her home in Belfast to Australia for years, ever since her sister moved there in the late 1970s.

"It was always in the back of my mind from when I was young. because I came here when I was nine," she explained. "My sister lives here. She moved here out of the Troubles. She was in a mixed marriage, Catholic-Protestant, so she emigrated here in 1977.

"I came to visit her in 1979 when I was only nine years of age, stayed here for six months with my mum and my brother.

My dad said, 'Oh, I'm not coming – I'm afraid of flying.' He wouldn't come out. We stayed here for six months in Perth and had a great time, loved it, went to school here, everything, and we were set up to stay here – only my dad wouldn't come. We had a job and everything lined up for him. He wouldn't come.

"But that's what it is. Your path's laid out for you. So I ended up going back [to Belfast]. From then I had it in my head, 'I'm emigrating. I'm going back to live in Australia with my sister and her family.'"

Gourley's home in Belfast during the Troubles – the nationalist conflict running across Ireland from the late 1960s into the 1990s – was defined by the military. The family's flat was in a block built on an old army barracks in a Republican area.

"There was a lot of shootings, a lot of bombings, and things like that, but as kids we didn't care at that stage, even though we were caught up in it. We just wanted to play in the streets, but I was the only girl that played with the boys," she recalled. She would join her younger brother and his friends playing football outside the building, and eventually progressing to a neighbouring piece of tarmac that had walls surrounding it, with a goal drawn on, enabling target practice. It might have been a step further on than playing in the street, but there were additional problems.

"It was just full of glass. So I remember going down with a brush, brushing the glass off, setting up," she said. It was at this point that Gourley's talent and drive for organisation began to make itself more evident. "Let's have a match with this other area! So we'd set up a game then."

Gourley's family eventually got a house and moved away from the block of flats, and she carried on playing with the boys in the new area, still with no other girls interested.

"I used to get the usual 'tomboy' – all the names. 'No, you're not playing,' or if you had a ball, 'Yeah, you can play' type of thing.

"There was nothing in the street, there was nowhere to play, and it was basically a thoroughfare, a road that we lived on, and it was a main road, so it was quite busy traffic, and we were just playing against an old gate post. So there was nothing else and we played against that."

As a teenager, Gourley grew away from football. Along with a local youth worker, she had tried to get other girls in the area together to set up a team, but their interest rapidly fizzled out. With no girls' team to play for, and unable to keep playing alongside the boys, other interests took priority, although she still watched football avidly as a supporter of Liverpool and a huge admirer of Kenny Dalglish. She left school and went to see her sister, spending time travelling around Australia, and then decided to return to Belfast, get a degree and take up a line of work. She got a youth work qualification and helped out in a local youth club, where the leader in charge told her that some of the girls were interested in playing football, and the hall would be free on a Sunday evening if she wanted to organise it.

"I used to go up with the girls, do a couple of kickabouts, a couple of drills, let them play. Then I started delving into it a wee bit more. Right, what's happening in Belfast? Is there any teams?"

There were no girls' teams. She found women's leagues, but nowhere for girls to play. Then she came across Belfast United, a cross-community team brought together by two women, one Catholic, one Protestant, who lived together and wanted to bring aspiring female players together regardless of faith, and entered teams into the local divisions. Gourley met one of the team's organisers and asked her what she should do with the youth club girls with nowhere to play.

"I said, 'What am I going to do with them? They really want to play football!'

"She said to me, 'Look, train them up, see how you go and then come into the divisions.'

"Honestly, these kids were only nine, ten, eleven, twelve, and we went in and played in this women's league."

The youth club team became Newington Girls, developing squads at different age levels. Gourley, along with others, went on to create the Northern Ireland Women's Football Association at a time when the primary football authorities across the world were not interested in supporting women to play the sport. She served as its secretary while continuing to coach, achieving her UEFA B licence while concluding her university study. She led the Northern Ireland schoolgirls' squads in representative tournaments, navigating a challenging line of negotiation with the Irish Football Association, managing to get kits from them only when the girls' teams were representing Northern Ireland within the Schools FA competitions.

"The IFA still were a hard wall to break down," she said. "We had to get in there and get them to recognise the girls."

Yet she thought back on those days of struggle with great fondness, admitting that her youth at the time – still in her twenties while she was part of the Northern Ireland Women's Football Association committee – had helped her find the drive and energy to keep fighting the battles.

"It was hard," she agreed. "I loved it. I loved what we were doing."

One of Gourley's players at Newington Girls was Marissa Callaghan, who went on to captain Northern Ireland. Gourley was naturally very proud of her international star, but was equally delighted with how many of her young players had progressed as they matured, not just as players but as people, and as new volunteers within the girls' and women's football space even if they were no longer in Belfast itself.

"Now they're all working, they've got their sports degrees same as mine, they're working in the industry, which is brilliant, and coaching," she said, adding that others were involved in the local community and continued to keep her updated on their progress, still grateful for her support and guidance during their younger years.

"I remember having to play football and driving through [military] barricades and girls hiding in the backseat of the car, and us cramming too many people in a car, cramming them in there because it was the only way we could get [them to matches]. Their parents didn't bring them, I had to go and ring their doorbells every Sunday morning to get them up for training or to get them out to go to games, and try and scrimp and save to maybe hire a minibus."

Callaghan was one of the players Gourley had managed to help on to a college scholarship in the USA, all thanks to contacts she had built up while volunteering, and it was one of the examples she pointed to when illustrating the power of sport.

"I loved what [the Northern Ireland Women's Football Association] were doing to drive the sport, to drive women's involvement, to empower these girls and women and say, 'Look, we don't care you're from working-class areas. We don't care you're from different sides of the community. Sport opens doors – just come out. There's opportunities. Just come out and play here. We want to get you involved and grow the game.'

"So that's what kept me going: the girls getting involved, the enjoyment of seeing them succeed as young females and go out and play for their country, or winning leagues.

"Those kids, if they hadn't had been saved by football, they were [perhaps] going to go down a rocky road or maybe not go to university – they wouldn't have went to university until we pushed them. They would have never known about scholarships to America until I started researching and then other women and people involved in the scene were telling me, 'This is what you do. Here's how you go about it.'"

Gourley got married when she was thirty and had her first daughter at the age of thirty-two, and it was then that she and her husband returned to the idea of emigrating. They had spent some time in Australia together during Gourley's degree, when she took a work placement and he got a year's working visa taking a variety of jobs. Now they were thinking of going back permanently, but it was a difficult decision to take, particularly uprooting little Catie from her grandparents, who doted on her.

"It was a really heart-wrenching decision to make," she admitted, "and we eventually decided yes, went through the application, and it only took two months for them to say, 'Yeah, here you go,' because with all my experience, points were not a problem: I had my degree, I was working in the area, he was a civil servant.

"So that was really quick. That was September and by December we were leaving."

As a sports development officer, Gourley became involved in the growth of girls' football in Australia almost immediately on arrival in 2007, both in her day job and, inevitably, as a volunteer and coach at her local team, Gosnells City FC. By the time Australia hosted the 2023 Women's World Cup, Gosnells had girls' teams from under-8s up to under-17s, plus a senior squad. She would not say so herself, of course, but it was in no small part down to Gourley. In the years since emigrating, she had gone into teaching, and had taken on the role of leading the soccer specialist programme at Lynwood Senior High School, with provision for both boys and girls – a real progression from her first months in post.

"I love what we've done for the girls. I used to have mixed classes; I used to take soccer specialist classes with some of the weaker boys and maybe five or six girls. Now we've got girls' [classes for] Year 7s, 8s, 9s, 10s, 11s and 12s, all soccer specialist classes. Girls love it."

That included Gourley's own daughters, Catie and Maria, both of whom had come through the Lynwood program. Catie had decided to pursue coaching qualifications and then go into studying health and physical education with a view to teaching, and specialising in football, just like her mother.

Her contributions to football were recognised when she was honoured with the national Coach of the Year award over the course of that World Cup summer.

"I was really embarrassed about it all, like, because I usually just go about doing my work, without fussing, but it was good to get that recognition," she said.

"My school were really proud of it, proud of me for doing that. I was really embarrassed. My principal at the time was like, 'Ann, this is brilliant,' because of the recognition the school got as well, so that was good.

"The whole euphoria around the World Cup, going to the games here, being involved in all that, our girls that were the flag-bearers and ball girls and things like that, they loved it. Loved it! And then we went across to Sydney and watched the semi-finals and finals. That was a very, very special year. Fantastic year."

Gourley bumped into Vanessa O'Brien through Donna Douglas – also a Gosnells player, but a former team-mate of O'Brien's at Manchester United. She was quickly roped into joining a Masters squad to compete at tournaments.

"We've been to Bali tournaments, we've been to the sevens

tournaments in Phuket, we've won that – played against teams from Hong Kong. Of course you get to Phuket, you're in the middle of playing these tournaments, teams from Hong Kong coming in, and Indonesia, and all you hear is, 'Ann! Gourley!' Somebody from Belfast. The girls are like, 'You can't go anywhere, walking through airports!' You see people you know, Singapore or Phuket or wherever you are, and you always meet somebody and it's all through football. How fantastic is that?"

FLIER

"I can't believe she got me all the way from England!"

Naz Ball was reflecting on her old friend and Wales team-mate Vanessa O'Brien's incredible powers of persuasion, getting her to fly halfway around the world to play in a Masters tournament in Bali.

"The girls couldn't believe it. They said, 'Where's Naz from?'

"'She's from England!'"

It had been a dramatic journey too, with her plane from Heathrow landing late into Kuala Lumpur, meaning a sprint across the airport to make the connecting flight. Her seatmate had told her, "I don't think you're going to make your connection," to which Ball responded: "I have to. I'm playing in a football tournament in Bali."

Ball's determination meant that despite the heat and humidity – and being dressed for UK weather rather than the conditions in her destination – she got her connecting flight, although her luggage did not make it. When she arrived at the hotel, she was looking forward to a lie-in ahead of two days of football.

"V[anessa] was laughing," Ball said. "'Oh yeah,' she goes. 'The tournament changed. We're only playing one day. We've got breakfast at six o'clock in the morning.'

"'V, I'm going to kill you!'"

Nevertheless, Ball made it in time the next morning, and the team enjoyed a great tournament, playing roll-on, roll-off substitutes in the sweltering heat.

"I hadn't done much exercise football-wise [before the tournament]. I played a lot of football that day – only one day. V and her husband were laughing at me over breakfast.

"'What's wrong with you?'

"'Everything aches!'"

Ball mimed a bow-legged stance, similar to the heroes of old Westerns and cowboy films, indicating great soreness.

"I was walking like John Wayne!"

Ball lived in Hemel Hempstead, Hertfordshire, a town on the commuter belt where the children playing on the greens scattered throughout the housing estates would likely don the club colours of local team Watford, or more probably a London club. Arsenal shirts were a common sight, and yet probably none of them knew that just around the corner was a woman whose name should have gone down in club history. Her playing career had come to a close too early for any genuine media spotlight, or for her achievements to be given the applause they deserved.

Naldra Ball – born in 1963 – and her six brothers grew up in north Wales, in the seaside resort of Pwllheli, and moved to Wigan at the age of twelve. Her nickname of "Naz" was bestowed on her when she played for Fodens Ladies for a season before joining the RAF.

At school, Ball found it difficult to learn because she was

not interested in the curriculum on offer. Her marks were not good, but she excelled in sport, representing the county in athletics. She knew that she did not want to stay at home in Wigan after leaving school, and it was by chance that she was in class when an RAF flight lieutenant came to speak to them.

Ball was intrigued, and went to speak to the officers at the careers information office in Manchester. She had to undergo fitness and aptitude tests, and joined the RAF officially on 12th March 1979, having turned eighteen on 28th February.

Ball headed to Hereford train station with the other new recruits and was met by the intimidating sergeant who would be overseeing their training.

"I wasn't naive because I came from Wigan, it was quite a rough area, but some of the girls were a bit softer, and their mum had mollycoddled them!" she laughed.

"The sergeant said, 'Right, from now on, [there'll] be no first name terms, it'll be Ball, and you address me as Sergeant. Yes, Sergeant, no, sergeant!'"

The sergeant told the girls to get in the minibus, adding: "I don't want anybody here that doesn't want to be here because if you don't want to be here you go back and your mum will do all your washing and ironing!"

Indeed, two of them stayed on the platform and got on the train back home.

Ball was allocated to C Flight, and completed her recruit training, including nuclear biological training ("how the hell I got through that!"), and trade training to enable her to work in catering.

"We went on exercises, and the men had 70 kg [in their packs] and the women had 70 kg. They just said, 'If you can't hack it then you're not going to be in the military,' so I had to get really fit. I think the fittest I was was when I went to the Falklands. I lost about two stone and came back with a six pack [of abs]."

Ball was posted to RAF Abingdon, and after a team in nearby Cuddington asked her to sign for them, she arranged with a friendly civilian contractor to cover her Sunday shifts so she could play matches. The team manager would pick her up from the camp in his big American car, or get one of her team-mates to shuttle her back and forth, or simply give her the cash for a taxi.

Between 1983 and 1986, after a spell in the Falklands, Ball was posted to Rheindahlen, West Germany. She wanted to keep playing football, and one of the RAF physical training instructors there – also a footballer – helped her to find a club. Historical accounts suggest that in the early part of the twentieth century, German authorities and media cracked down hard on the renegade women who wanted to play football; historian Jean Williams reports that in 1920, a team in Frankfurt decided to take up rowing instead of facing the ongoing gauntlet of public ridicule. Yet women did continue to organise themselves, and by 1955, even though the men's governing bodies refused to recognise women's teams, they created the German Ladies' Football Association, organising domestic and international matches. Despite initially putting forward some modified rules to make the game less 'rough' for female players, West Germany's federation, the DFB, were one of the first of UEFA's members to begin to support the women's game at the start of the 1970s, allowing women's teams to play double-headers and take to the pitch prior to men's matches, but that did not mean an immediate overhaul. Instead, they continued to allow the existing regional set-ups to run their competitions before taking on the operation of a nationwide league in 1973/74.

First Ball signed for Wiedenbrück, who played in the second tier, but were what she described as "a fun club, not really serious about football", although she was quick to praise: "The way they treated footballers, female footballers, was just something else." She moved on later to Frauen-Bundesliga club Lövenich, which shared all their facilities with their men's side.

"I just thought, 'Well, this is a really good club,' and training was great. And the girls were very disciplined."

It did take her a while to settle in, with her new team-mates slightly wary of the interloper.

"They were bit offish with me for a while, and I thought, 'Well, I'm bloody staying, you're not getting rid of me.' It took me about a year to get accepted by the girls, and once they knew I was staying and I was probably a decent footballer, then the whole ethos changed and I became part of the squad and the girls used to talk to me in English when they hadn't talked to me in English before! I said, 'You buggers!' They said, 'Oh, we thought you were going to leave, Naz!' So they did put me under a lot of pressure."

Playing in a foreign country, where she did not speak the language, and of course had her work responsibilities as well, was a tough challenge. She watched the training sessions closely and copied everything as much as she could, because she could not understand the instructions in German.

"It was very difficult. Yeah, I found it really, really hard. But I just stuck with it, and just went and looked at what the players were doing and just followed suit. I was never at the front because I didn't know what the hell the manager was telling me, so I used to step back and just watch.

"Once all the girls accepted me then they would [translate], but I was a centre forward. When you're in a team and you're a centre forward, it's quite easy to know what you need to be doing. Just put the ball in. Just score, Naz, that's all we want you to do. My fitness was phenomenal."

So passionately did Ball love football that she played in the RAF catering team as the only woman alongside a squad of men. Gaining their acceptance was possibly marginally easier than being welcomed in Germany, but it was still a challenge.

"The first time I presented myself – because I'm only small – the men went, 'What the bloody hell is this woman doing here?'

"'I've turned up for training! It's a training session, a football training session!'

"The coach said, 'Right, come on, somebody needs to partner Naz.'"

She gestured to indicate the silence which met the coach's call.

"I stuck it out. I said, 'I'm just going to carry on training, I need to get fit.' There were a lot of fit girls at Arsenal as well, so you have to keep on top of it, you just can't train two weeks [pre-season] and then [not bother], you need to put extra work in, so I did an extra session with the lads.

"Then eventually after about five months, [the coach said,] 'All right, guys, let's get together.'

"'Yeah, I'll partner Naz!'

"'Yeah, I'll partner her, no worries at all!'

"So I got partners. The guys then [admitted], 'Oh, Naz is not a bad footballer for a girl.'"

By 1987, when Ball returned to the UK, Cuddington – and players in the Buckinghamshire area – got taken under the wing of Vic Akers, the Arsenal Ladies manager and club kitman, a huge champion for women's football. In the 1980s, a women's team sharing a men's club's name invariably fell under their community outreach programme.

"We had the facilities of the old Arsenal, the ball court and the old JVC [Centre, an indoor facility at the Gunners' Highbury home]. The only thing I can remember was training was so tough. They wouldn't let us on the pitch because that was sacred. It wasn't for the women. It was only for the men.

"Where the gravel was around the pitch, we did our training there. Vic had us in the stands, down corridors, running, we had to go to the park, we did loads, we had the bleep test – we had all that!"

The newly christened Arsenal Ladies were run particularly well for the time, especially because they had some access to limited resources, although they had to play their matches at the Hare and Hounds ground in Walthamstow, but they were still amateur. Post-match teas were provided by players (with Ball's catering experience coming in very handy), each drawing a refreshment item out of a hat to bring. Squad members would car-share and give each other petrol money.

"If we were playing Everton or Liverpool or Doncaster on a Sunday – I don't think we had any Saturday games – then you would get up early, meet wherever you needed to meet, people picked you up, drive up – which is, what, Liverpool then? Three-hour drive – played football.

"And some of the pitches, you wouldn't put pigs on them. Changing rooms were bad, wooden huts and cold water, no hot water.

"We didn't have a lot, really, and all our kit was [paid for by] parents or relatives or friends or RAF people: 'I'll sponsor your socks a tenner, Naz', whatever it was. Nothing off Arsenal. Took them a while to get going."

Attached to a well-known men's club, and with access to good facilities even if the money invested into the women's team was limited, Arsenal attracted many good players, meaning there was significant competition for places. If one player did not want to make the effort to travel or train, then there would be several others ready to step into her place; even if she was injured, she would try her hardest to return to action and reclaim her shirt as soon as possible.

"We always knew, though, at Arsenal, as we started to get strength in depth and more players in, I always thought that I had to do that extra training to keep in the squad, and I didn't want to get injured because there was girls knocking on the door for your place, so I always did that little bit of extra training to make sure I fit in, and I very rarely missed training.

"My missus used to say, 'You're not going, it's bloody snow!' or 'It's pelting it down with rain, you're going to go training tonight?!'

"'Yeah. I'm just going to get wet!'

"One night it was snowing, and I still turned up, we still trained, I think they had us run the running track. We had a good team strength in depth then, so you had to just do that little bit extra because I always knew if I got injured one or two good players would be coming through, so you were always under pressure, which I think is a good thing really. You're not then thinking, 'I'm a great player.' That was the good thing about Vic, he kept everyone on their toes. It was good, that squad, a good squad of girls."

In the final years of Ball's playing career, she represented Wembley Ladies. Although she didn't like the phrase itself, she had become a bit-part player for Arsenal, coming on as substitute for the last twenty minutes, and she wanted to get some genuine game time. She was approached by Wembley manager John Jones, who invited her to join his team, and she broke the news to Arsenal boss Akers.

"He said, 'Yeah, yeah, Naz. If that's what you want to

do.' So he let me go. Fair enough. I probably thought I had another year left in me.

"But my old mate who played midfield, she said, 'Naz, it was so funny, the team talk in the changing rooms when we played Wembley: Vic always used to say, I want somebody on Naz Ball! Man-to-man marking her! She's going to be the danger!'

"And my mate was telling me everyone was laughing in the changing rooms. 'Why the hell didn't you give her a go?!'

"I stayed two years with Wembley. I loved it. I thought I did really well there."

Of course, attached to a club with such a famous footballing name, and with the team enjoying great success, there was the occasional moment of media interest. Ball remembered vividly a music video with a leading pop group of the time, and a photo shoot for a now-defunct tabloid newspaper. She had been under the impression that it would be a fashion-focused spread in a supplement, and was excited at the prospect of trying on some expensive designer clothes. The reality was somewhat different.

"We were all in a row and had our make-up on, our lipstick on," she remembered, "with stockings on, ra-ra skirts and tops and everything."

Indeed, looking back at the newspaper archive, Ball's memory was spot-on; in the background of the photo, on the scoreboard, the illuminated text reads: "Wembley Ladies FC, Euro Girlies 96", suggesting that the news angle for the tabloid was to tie in with the forthcoming men's European

Championships in England that summer. The players themselves are indeed all in a row, with red cropped tops and short
white skirts, and each woman's leg nearest the camera slightly
lifted and bent at the knee, similar to a can-can dancer. It may
have been the biggest mainstream media coverage Wembley
Ladies got during that period, but it was hardly indicative of
them being taken seriously as gifted footballers.

"I said, 'I am not putting that on,' and they said, 'Naz,
you've got to put it on!'

"I don't wear a skirt. Lipstick, you're joking me? Heels?
Fishnet stockings-type thing? Oh, my God. We were just,
'We've got to do it – it's for the newspapers.'"

Ball's Wales call-up came relatively late into her career, with no
official national team prior to that. The set-up she encountered
was far from what she had been used to with her club sides, with
domestic football in Wales comparatively weak, and a relatively
small player pool to be selected from. It was no wonder that the
management cast their nets wider, looking for players beyond
the country's borders who would qualify for Wales.

"I was lucky because [I was] playing for Arsenal, and
Vanessa [O'Brien] was at Leasowe Pacific and she was in a
good team. But I always find a little bit of resentment because
they'd forget, they'd say, 'Oh, yeah. You play for a team in
London. You play for Arsenal and you're a southerner.'

"I'd say, 'No, I'm not a southerner, I was born in North
Wales and quite proud to be Welsh, and when I put that shirt
on I'm probably more Welsh than some of you players. I was
born and bred in north Wales, and I'm Welsh.'"

She was also not impressed with the pitches they were given to play on ("not brilliant", she said with understatement) or the kit ("awful, because we were second- or third-rate citizens"). Just as O'Brien remembered, Ball also recalled the failure to provide them with kit that actually fitted them, and vividly recollected the static electricity generated by the synthetic fibres. She was pleased that in the years since her playing career, the Wales football authorities had recognised their early representatives, but hoped they might do more. She mentioned that although former players had been invited to significant matches, they were not welcomed in the same way that corporate guests were; the last time she had travelled from Hertfordshire to Wales for an international, paying for her own travel, on arrival at the ground she had been given a voucher for a free drink, but the only catering laid on was for the corporate suites. Still, the fact that there was recognition of former players at all, let alone corporate suites, was indicative of a lot of change in the women's game.

"I'm glad the ladies' game has changed for the better. People say, 'Naz, you'd be worth a fortune [in transfer fees now],' and I just think we've forgotten not just me but a lot of really good footballers – we're like forgotten heroes really. Where did Arsenal start? Nobody's ever asked me that.

"They'll say, 'Naz Ball?'"

She imitated a blank look of ignorance.

"I'll say, 'Well, I scored lots and lots of goals for Arsenal, I was a centre forward. I used my head. I was a proper little poacher. I wasn't a versatile centre forward like now you've got to do, it's more hard work, because you've got to come and support more, I think, whereas before they just said, 'Naz, you stay in the box, we'll put the ball in the box, you head the ball!'"

Although she admired her friend and former team-mate Vanessa O'Brien's politeness and positivity when it came to reflecting on the past, she was committed to brutal honesty.

"A lot of people sit on the fence, don't they? No, you have to tell the truth. What was ladies' football like?"

Of course, she said, neither the standard nor the organisation were as good then as the modern game, but she pointed out that in the second half of her footballing career, twice a week she would work a full day on the early shift, then go to training, which would finish at Highbury at 10 p.m. She would then have a shower, and go back to her base at Bentley Priory in Stanmore Park, north-west London, getting to bed at around midnight.

"That's for the love of football. We never thought about money. We did the food [after the games]. We had great supporters. We didn't get anything in return, but we did it because of our love for football. That's what it all was about."

She compared the swift progress of women's football in England to the forward-thinking set-up she had found in Germany in the 1980s.

"It was so professionally run, you just felt wanted, you know. Special, that's the word. A few of the girls at the time were some of the German [national team] players. They had sponsorship and were driving [sponsored] cars round, that far ago."

She likened the contrast to the German beers that were on sale then, only now available in UK supermarkets, and considered brand-new to British observers; the German league had been providing its players with recognition, respect and resources decades ago, and only recently had the English league caught up.

"I was drinking that twenty years ago, that's gone out, mate!" she laughed. "Twenty years ago! You're telling me this new beer's supposed to have [just] come out?! Football's a bit like that, in a way."

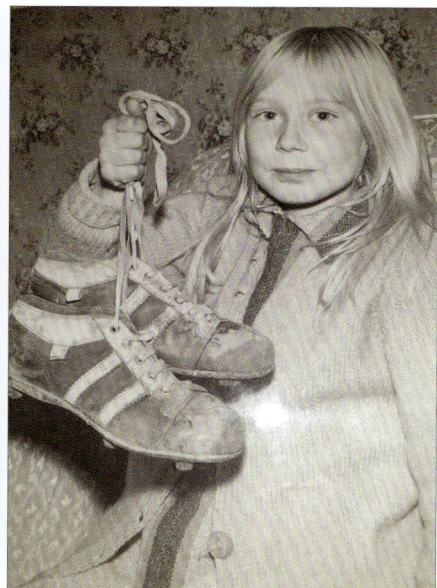

Childhood photo of
Jeannie Allott

Jeannie Allott's
legacy cap

Hammarby fans hail Karen Farley's
historic goal (*Photo: Henric Wauge*)

Karen Farley with
her nephew Conor

Edna Neillis featured in the national newspapers following her ban
(*courtesy of Elsie Cook*)

Edna Neillis in the front row, far left, with Gorgonzola
(*courtesy of Elsie Cook*)

Issy Pollard in action

Sian Williams, second from left, front row

Photo on the wall of Naz Ball's house from her Arsenal days
(*photo taken by the author*)

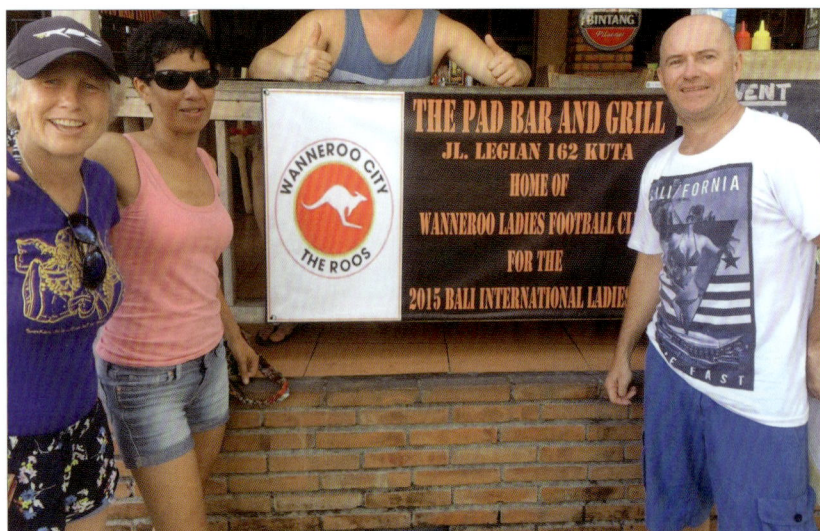

Naz Ball, Vanessa O'Brien and husband Todd
at the 2015 Bali tournament

PART TWO

*Playing every other day is obviously very difficult for us.
Germans and other European countries are more used to it than
we are. Maybe that's what we've got to look to in the future.*
                    Debbie Bampton, England captain, 13th June 1995

SUPPORTER

"I find it really hard to talk about myself and my achievements. I'm more interested in helping others and developing others."

Louise Newstead, the head of coaching at the PFA (the Professional Footballers' Association, the union for players in England), had dedicated the majority of her adult life to supporting other people's progress in football.

Before taking on the role, she had spent six years as a regional coach developer for them, working under her mentor Jim Hicks, going into professional clubs and delivering coaching education to their young players, professional players and their staff. At the time she began the role, the only fully professional clubs in the country were men's clubs.

Prior to that, she worked for Millwall Community Trust, stepping full-time into the world of football as a girls' and women's development officer, coaching in the local community and setting up a structure so they could compete in competitions, ultimately leading to the establishment of the country's first-ever girls' centre of excellence, a model that was later adopted by the FA and rolled out more widely.

Her coaching and strategic credentials were impeccable, and she had vast experience in the men's and boys' game. Very few people with whom she worked knew that, as Lou Waller, she had been one of Millwall Lionesses' stars, representing England at the 1995 Women's World Cup.

"I don't sit there and say what I've done, so a lot of my colleagues, for a long, long time, they didn't even know my playing background. Jim might mention it in conversation and then my colleagues would go, 'Lou, you played for England?' And I'm like, 'Yeah.' And so they'd ask you questions but even now when we're on courses, a lot of my colleagues will share their background and they now go, 'Listen, she won't tell you, but she's done x, y and z.' People will come up to me maybe midway through the course, six months into the course, and go, 'They've just told me that you played for England!' or 'You played x amount of games for Millwall!' and I'm like, 'Yeah, I have.' If they've found out they've most probably had to go and find out themselves."

Waller had grown up as a Millwall fan, and at the age of eighteen she was scouted by Lionesses former manager Alan Wooler, who was playing professionally in Finland. Top Finnish club HJK, based in the capital Helsinki, wanted English players to join their squad, and invited Waller and team-mate Maureen Jacobson to Monaco to play in a tournament with them. They won it, and soon afterwards Waller got a phone call inviting her to join HJK on a semi-professional basis.

"It was as good as professional, because all I was doing was playing football and getting paid for it.

"Back in the day, you didn't have agents. I was working. I had a good job, really good job for somebody of such a young

age. And I was just like, 'Yeah, but I want to play football.'
So my dad was, as ever, a support. He just said, 'Listen, if
that's what you want to go and do, I'd rather you go and do
it and look back, than look back and go, I wish I'd done it.'"

At that time, Waller was an executive officer in the civil
service, one of the youngest to be appointed in the role, so
it was really no wonder that she described her manager as
"gobsmacked" at the news that she was leaving.

"He said, 'What is it you're going to go and do, then?' And
I said, 'I'm going to go and play football.' He was just like,
'You're what?!'

"'Yeah, I'm going to go and play football in Finland!'

"He was like, 'Are you sure you're making the right decision?' I just was like, 'It's really what I want to go and do.'
So, yeah, so I left."

At the age of eighteen, Waller was leaving her close-knit
family and the football club she loved to play football and get
paid for it, something she never thought would happen to her.

"There wasn't a career in the game for a female, whether
it be playing or coaching. There wasn't females around the
game, so I went over there and I got paid, I got an apartment, I got a car. I would eat in restaurants: I would only
have my breakfast at home, but I would go to a restaurant
for my lunch, and they would really look after you, and then
I would go to another restaurant for dinner, and that's what
it would be like, the whole week. I'd get paid but I couldn't
really spend my money, because I didn't have to spend it on
anything!"

Women's football had been officially played in Finland since 1971, and taken into the national set-up the year after. At the start of the 1980s, there were around 3,000 female players in the country, explaining why ambitious teams looking for top-quality individuals might have to look beyond their borders. As with other Scandinavian countries, the scheduling of the season from late spring to early autumn permitted British players to return to the UK in September or October, if they wished, and play for a club there. It was a tempting proposition.

HJK's women's team was affiliated to the men's. Those players who were not on the same kind of contract as Waller tended to work for companies who were linked to the club, meaning they would work early in the day, and then leave to go to training in the afternoon. The women trained at the facilities next to the main stadium, and played their home matches either on the training pitch or the main ground. If the team had an away game that was in the northern part of Finland, they would fly up, although Waller was never entirely happy about getting on the small plane they used: "I don't mind flying, but every time I got on there, I was like, 'Please, please let this thing land.'"

With strong financial support, the team had everything they needed, as far as Waller was concerned.

"If we didn't have a game that weekend, they would arrange for us to go off to a summer cottage, cottages that they owned, and we would go there, and it was a team bonding thing that you would do.

"You'd go to the Adidas warehouse, and I literally always remember them just sliding the doors [open]. They would just go, 'This, this, this, this and this' – bearing in mind I'm coming from a playing era where our kits didn't fit us, we always got the men's kits, they were big and baggy.

"They were as professional as you could be at that time. But going over and doing pre-season, God, I thought I was going to die. They had us running in the woods. Everything out there is very kind of fitnessy, they have trails through the woods. The training, it was intense, but then they would look after you off the pitch – you'd have to go and have regular massages, you were definitely booked in at minimum once a week, twice a week. The off-pitch care was there as well."

The number of Finnish people fluent in English helped Waller to settle in swiftly, but she was a little embarrassed that she did not pick up too much of the native language herself.

"It's one of the most difficult languages. Somebody was telling me a lot of words have got seventeen different endings depending in what context you're using them. So I'd learn a little bit, around numbers and stuff that I needed on the football pitch. But most of the time, yeah, my teammates, they would just be like, 'Lou, speak to me in English,' because they get taught [it], they have to learn English, they have to learn German, and can actually converse in those languages."

In fact, she felt so at home so quickly that it rather surprised her as well, as her family. Prior to signing for HJK, she had been away from home once before, on a school skiing trip, and had got herself so worked up and anxious about missing home that her father had had to talk her down.

"I was a real homer, I like being at home with my family," she said. "But I was fine [in Finland]. I think I just absolutely loved it so much. My parents, they would come out and visit, and they always said to me, 'If things get too much, you want to go home for a few days, not a problem' – they would pay for all my flights to come back.

"Not that I did. In the end, my mum used to phone up, and go, 'Is there any chance of you calling us?!' I'd be like, 'Yeah!'"

Waller would fly over for England camps – paid for by her club – and at the end of the Finnish season would rejoin Millwall Lionesses before going back out to Helsinki.

"That [England] squad was a fixed squad. To get in now, people are in and out of the England squad. They rack up caps. [Then], you had to be in that squad a very, very long time, and because we didn't play that many games, it was hard to break in. So I was training with the senior team, I played with the under-18s, and then they set up a loose [under-]21s. I made my debut for the women's England senior team in '89 and I was [first] out in Finland in '88 so there was a bit of a crossover, but it was fine, because whenever I got selected to come for training, then my Finnish team, no questions, would release me. They would fly me over, and they would fly me back. In those early days, if I was going up to Lilleshall [for England camp], I was paying that expense to go and play for my country, but [HJK] covered absolutely everything for me."

She had nothing but praise for then-England manager Martin Reagan, who was supportive of her career in Finland, accepting that if she was training and playing she would be match-fit, even if he could not watch her in club action regularly, and was open to discussion if there were any issues around her travel.

"The best way to describe him: he was a gentleman. Honestly, he was one of the best guys I've ever, ever met or played under. This whole thing now [in coaching], it's very much about 'don't just develop the player, but also develop the person'. Well, he was way, way ahead of his years, because he was always concerned first and foremost about you the person. He recognised if he could get that right and get you in a good place, then that gave him the platform to get the very best out of you as a player. I could pick up the phone and speak to him about anything. Good and bad, you could speak to Martin, and you knew that he would listen and he wouldn't hold it against you, and you knew that you could speak to him in confidence."

Although she loved playing in Finland, as she turned twenty she began to rethink whether it was a genuine long-term plan – describing it as "a sensible moment". Having returned to England after the Finnish season, she was considering whether she ought to gain some more qualifications to add to the O-levels she had achieved at school.

"I was like, 'Lou, you can't [keep doing this]. You've left school at sixteen, you've gone to work. You've gone over to Finland to play football, you're having a great life. But reality is, you can't play football forever, so what are you going to do? Because if you were to come back in your mid-twenties, what have you got?'"

She found a course in sport she liked at Southwark College, and decided she would complete that and then go back to HJK.

"I said to them, 'Look, this is the situation, this is why.' They went, 'We understand. Not a problem. We don't want you to go. Your contract is there. Do your course, finish your course, and then come and re-sign.' And I was like, 'Right, fine.'"

By a huge stroke of coincidence, Waller's tutor on the course was Brent Hills. He had played non-league football and trained as a PE teacher, before going on to coach at various clubs and later to serve as assistant coach and then caretaker England manager. That was all more than a decade in the future at this point, though; he was lecturing at the college and supported Waller through her Level 2 coaching badge. He encouraged her to coach the staff football team as well as stage a session for the students, and she extended her skills with a role at the Millwall Community Trust, who continued to lead the way in offering coaching and a playing pathway for girls.

"They were doing some stuff around trying to promote girls' football, so I would go in [to schools and groups] and be a bit of a role model, doing a bit of coaching.

"Then what they said to me was, 'Lou, we're going to advertise a job as a girls' and women's football development, one of the very first in the country. We'd be really keen for you to apply.'

"And I was like, 'Yeah, but I want to go back to Finland to play football.'"

Assuming she would not get the job, she decided to apply anyway. Then she discovered she had been successful and was left at a tricky crossroads.

"I was like, 'What do I do here?' This is an opportunity here for me to work in football, develop girls' football, something that I was really passionate about because of the opportunities it had given me up until that stage in my life. It was for my club Millwall, and I love Millwall to bits. I'm a Millwall fan. I'm playing for the women's team. I was like, 'No, I've got to give this a go.'

"So I had to speak to my guys in Finland, and again, they were brilliant, and they just said, 'Listen, if it doesn't work out, you will always have a place here. We'd have you back at the drop of a hat.'"

Waller stayed with Millwall Community Trust for twenty-five years, a role she loved for giving her the chance to coach full-time in the area in which she grew up, giving something back to the club and the community that she felt had given her so much. She also volunteered her time to coach in other local groups, enabling her to create her own network to identify talented girl players and help them to begin playing at a club.

Waller even joined the Millwall Lionesses club committee, serving as chair for a time. This was before a difficult period where the women's team playing in the elite second tier of competition broke away from the men's club, ultimately rebranding as London City Lionesses, leaving those at Millwall to begin to restructure their pathway to senior women's football. Waller stepped away from the club at around this time, devoting her energy instead to her family, especially her two young sons. After a break of around six years, she returned to coaching, but in boys' football. She chose her work carefully, particularly when she was asked to work with girls' teams; she would coach only at clubs where she shared their values and principles and felt that they were treating their players well.

After a quarter of a century at Millwall Community Trust, Waller moved on in 2018 to the PFA, taking on a high-profile senior role as head of coach development in 2024. As always, she was thinking about the impact her career might possibly have on the next generations.

"It's a brilliant opportunity that I've got, and it's a very, very high profile job, and the fact that I'm female as well…"

She paused. "For me, people have to go first and break down barriers and achieve things so that others that follow can actually believe, 'You know what? There's potential for me to go and do that as well.' I think it's an unbelievable opportunity that's been afforded to me in the game, and one that I hope would make a difference to other females that [will] maybe consider a career of that nature in the future."

SETTLER

After England were knocked out of the 1995 Women's World Cup at the quarter-final stage, the squad headed from Västerås – where the 3-0 defeat to Germany was staged, around 100 kilometres west of Stockholm – back to Sweden's capital, ready for their journey. One player was already home: Karen Farley, who by this time had already spent three years playing her football there.

"We were given three hours to go and explore the city, and then [I said to] our little group, 'We're doing this, let's go down to the harbour and see if we can get someone to take us out on a boat. Let's get a few pints!'

"We were all in our England tracksuits and everything, and I sweet-talked some bloke on this beautiful little wooden boat down in Stockholm harbour to take us out. We all had a great time."

As many other England players of the time experienced, the squads were – as Farley put it – "ruled with an iron fist". She recalled a time when she and her closest friends in the squad had been scolded for their conduct, and she maintained that they had not done anything wrong.

"We were just laughing, having a good time, and we got summonsed and they told us that we were absolutely disgraceful, our behaviour was disgraceful, the things that we were doing were not acceptable, we were representing our country."

Decades on, the attitude of some of the England hierarchy still puzzled her. "It was almost like you had to be so grateful that you were doing this. It was like they expected robots. I remember we always used to be like, 'Do the men get treated like this?'"

Having looked back at some of the match coverage she had recorded from English television during that Women's World Cup, her opinions on the tone used to the players by coaches and media alike had not changed either.

"I used to stand there and think, '[Do they] not realise that we've all played football all of our lives, and we know football?' The actual tactical side of things wasn't really the problem, our main issue was fitness."

Watching modern-day international women's football with her daughter, the memories of her own time playing at the top level were very clear – for example, the emphasis placed on the national anthem.

"[My daughter] was like, 'Did you sing?' And I was like, 'Did I sing? We had to. We were told. We had to sing.'

"I mean, there was no way I wouldn't have sung, but we were told before we went out for a game. It was like, 'You will sing the national anthem. Do not dare to not sing the national anthem.' It was like those things were really important. The fact that that we couldn't keep up with anyone on the pitch was almost second."

Farley found these mindsets particularly restrictive as she was used to being a professional footballer in Sweden, where they treated their female footballers with respect. By 1980, they boasted the fourth-largest participation in women's football in Europe, with 9,400 registered players in a national population of only roughly eight million; four years later they won the inaugural Women's European Championships. It was a long way – literally and figuratively – from her weekday admin job in central London and her weekends playing for Millwall Lionesses. She was living in a flat in a Victorian house conversion in South Norwood, London, and she had noticed her new neighbours were less than salubrious.

"I was just like, 'What am I doing here?' and I literally went to training on a Tuesday night, and the trainer at the time was like, 'Do you want to go to Sweden and play football?'

"'Do I want to what?'

"'Do you want to go to Sweden and play football?'

"'I don't understand the question. What are you talking about?'

"'Well, there's a team in Sweden, they want a forward, and I think you'd be great. I think you'd do a great job out there.'

"And I was like, 'Yeah, all right then, yeah.'"

As with her team-mate Lou Waller, it was Alan Wooler who had made the suggestion of making the move. One of his friends owned a business that sponsored Lindsdals IF, who were without two of their first-choice forwards in the midst of their quest for promotion to the top league. Farley went to work the next day and took a week's annual leave, then packed her kit bag.

"I didn't have a clue where I was going. I mean, Sweden: Abba, Björn Borg, that was it. I didn't know where it was, didn't know anything. I had to fly via Copenhagen so I came into Copenhagen, I had to get on a little propeller aeroplane over to Kalmar [where the team were based]. I didn't know where I was going, what I was doing, what to expect, I didn't know anyone."

She was met at the airport by a club representative holding up a sign with her name on. Farley, at the age of twenty, might have felt confused, but all who followed Lindsdals felt nothing but delight at her arrival, sure that this new English striker would be the solution to all their problems.

"I've still got all the paper clippings from the local newspapers where it was like, 'The superstar from England is coming over to save us!' and all this. It was crazy. I spent a week there on a trial, played a couple of games, did a few training sessions, and then they said, 'We'll let you know.' I was home a day or two, and they rang and they said, 'Yeah, we want you to come, we want you to come and play the season.'"

Immigration laws at the time meant Farley had to apply for a visa and a work permit, which stated her profession as football player. She gave up her admin job without a second thought, and nor did anyone in her life suggest that she should think about her decision a little more carefully.

"There was never any, 'Are you sure you're doing the right thing?' [from my parents] – nothing like that. And the friends that I had at the time were really just football friends, and they were all just: 'Well, go on then, go for it.' So everyone was just quite supportive."

She considered.

"I don't even know if I want to say supportive. I didn't really care, to be honest with you, I really didn't care. I just saw it as a way out, a way out of the life that I was living at that time and using something that I could do. I didn't even have to try to play football. It just came so naturally that it was like, 'Shit, someone wants me to go out there and do that. I get to live in a different country!'

"When I look back now, I think, 'Fucking hell.' The naivety of youth is just so beautiful, isn't it? If someone were to come now and say, 'Do you want to go?' I'll be like, 'Oh no.' But at that stage, I didn't care about anything. All I could see was that it was an opportunity. I'd get to go and play football, and just play football all the time, and it was just fantastic. I got to make so many new friends, I learned a new language, I learned a new culture, and that still sits with me now."

Farley settled into life in Sweden swiftly, never experiencing homesickness, and keeping her trips back to visit family and friends brief as she simply preferred being in her new home in Kalmar, a small town in the south-east of the country, and finding it almost unbelievable the way that women's football was treated.

"I was famous when I went there, it was ridiculous. I remember I would walk down the street, and people, little kids, would come running up to me and be asking for my autograph and everything. I was like…" She mimed open-mouthed shock. "What is this place? I've come from playing for Millwall, we won the FA Cup and everything, but nobody knew anything unless you were involved in football. But here, it was crazy."

Moving to Hammarby was a step up even from the star treatment she got at Lindsdals.

"We were on the front page in the newspapers all the time, but still nowhere near where it is now. But we got sponsorship, we got given our kit, we got given our boots, we had access to a physio. It was night and day in comparison to England at the time."

At Hammarby, Farley found that she had only Wednesday evenings and Sundays free; she trained every other night with a match on Saturday. By now fluent in Swedish, she also worked at the British Embassy alongside her football. It was perhaps no wonder that she was so happy in Sweden.

"When it came to any equality, just in general, I never experienced any kind of sexism or anything derogatory in Sweden. I never experienced that. You were just hyped up, and if you were good then obviously even more. Going to Sweden was life-changing for me in so many ways, not just football. It really changed my life."

It was partly that Sweden as a country gave Farley what she perceived later as somewhere she could understand and be herself. She found it difficult to grow up gay in Britain, where lesbianism or homosexuality in general was never mentioned, although in football she was accepted and never questioned or judged.

"I was born in 1970, so my teenage years were the 80s when being gay was just not a thing. The fear of being found out that you were gay was just so enormous. I remember when I first started playing football, I was ten when I first started playing football, but obviously, at that age, you have no clue [about your sexuality], and then as I got older and started realising that I was gay, it was my safe space. You never got any grief, there were other gay people that played, you could be yourself.

"When I went to Sweden, even over there, there weren't really that many gay players in the team that I was in, but nobody gave a shit, basically. You've been given that freedom to just be who you are. Sweden was almost an escape for me, because it was completely accepted over in Sweden, whereas here in England, homosexuality was just like so frowned upon. It was wrong. That's all I ever used to hear: 'Oh, you play football, oh, you bloody lesbian.' It's like, 'God, why? OK, so that's wrong then? Am I bad then, am I?'

"Football gave me that space to be me and feel comfortable and not be ashamed of who I was. I was really good at football, and I was supported for that, and people celebrated me for being that footballer who was gay and no one gave a shit, because I was good at football."

Farley's England career began thanks to the proactivity of her Hammarby coaches Paul Balsom and Pia Sundhage, who put together a clips package of her performances and sent the video to Ted Copeland via the FA.

"I didn't even know about it," she said. "I remember getting the letter, getting the call-up and calling [Balsom] and saying, 'I've just been called up to England!'

And he was like, 'Thank God for that. I'm not surprised, I sent them a video saying you need to know that you've got this player that's over here in the Swedish league, dominating the Swedish league, scoring all these goals, and you need to know about her.'

"They didn't have a clue."

That first call-up came in December 1994, for a European Championship semi-final against Germany at Vicarage Road, Watford, and she went straight into the starting line-up without having been part of a training camp beforehand. This was a crucial game in a tournament that stretched over several months, with home and away legs, rather than the intense group stage and knock-out rounds that football fans may be more used to. Germany had won two of the previous five editions, so everyone involved with the England team knew that they would present a tough challenge. It was no wonder that Farley was extremely nervous. She recalled second-guessing how much she should talk to these new team-mates, and remembered Sian Williams being particularly welcoming to her.

"I remember coming to the first England camp and walking in and just being so desperately nervous, even though I'd grown up playing with most of these players. But it was people like Hope Powell, Marieanne Spacey and Debbie Bampton and Gill Coultard and all of these people: you're like, 'Fucking hell!' These are your heroes that you have looked up to, so it was very scary."

Farley's experience of high intensity and high professionalism in Sweden also meant she was now out of practice at doing things the English way.

"I knew that I was doing things the way I did them in Sweden, and it just wasn't like that in England. They'd be like, 'How often do you train?'

"'Four times a week!'

"I remember the first time I went to training in Sweden, and the warm-up, I was like, 'Have we got to play a game after this?' because the warm-up was just so intense. I'm like, 'Nah, this is more than our pre-season training [in England]!' Training sessions here, you couldn't compare them."

She added: "Coming back to an England camp [for me] – it was like taking a step back."

Several England players from a variety of eras had struggled to make their mark internationally if they were playing overseas; many of them felt that if they were not in the English domestic league, the England coach did not even consider them. That was not the case for Farley, who had not been on the England radar prior to her move to Sweden, despite having played for the junior international teams.

"They probably didn't even know that I'd gone abroad! They wouldn't have any clue. I just left Millwall, went off and played football. There was nothing. There was no contact."

The video courtesy of Hammarby was enough to wake the England coaches up to her potential, hence putting her straight in despite never having seen her play in person. It paid swift dividends as she scored in the seventh minute of the match.

"They were obviously like: 'Well, that's all right, then! That paid off, didn't it?' I played that game, went back to Sweden. No contact [from England], no nothing. There was never any follow-up. There was never any, 'How's it going? How's your fitness? Are you doing this?' No programmes to follow. No 'how you doing with your food? How you doing with it?' Nothing. There was nothing. I literally would come home, I would play a game, I would go back to Sweden, and I wouldn't hear anything until the next time a letter dropped on my mat saying, 'We've got another game, we're playing so and so, you need to be here at this time.'"

Farley got her last cap in February 1996, at the age of twenty-five, marking the end of a senior international career that lasted only two years, with eleven appearances and eight goals. The premature end was partly due to an anterior cruciate ligament injury, but she thought her England career should perhaps have started earlier.

"The ACL injury cut everything short. I mean, I'm probably not blowing my own trumpet, but should have been there two or three years earlier, probably when I first went out to Sweden, but there just wasn't that contact.

"They had no idea how I was playing in Sweden. The only important thing was when I came back and played for England, that I did a good job, and that's why I got called back again."

Farley, now married and a mother of two, looked at the societal landscape today and marvelled at how different it was for her children compared to her own teenage years.

"This whole 'they/them' thing that goes on now [with people opting to use non-gendered pronouns], I would always talk about people using 'they' and 'them'.

"'Did you go out at the weekend?'

"'Yeah, went out with a friend. They were really good, yeah, no, we had a really good time there. They are really nice.'

"I used to use 'they' because I couldn't ever say it, I didn't want to say 'she', or 'her', or whatever, you just hid it. It was scary. It was really scary.

"I think, 'Oh, how wonderful, the freedom that these young kids [nowadays] have to just be who they want to be.' But yes, football certainly saved me."

She was also glad that female players now had the liberty to talk about their lives without feeling the need to conceal any of it, praising former Arsenal team-mates Beth Mead and Vivianne Miedema for being public about their relationship. She scorned the idea that it was unnecessary for any athlete to talk about their partner or relationship status.

"It's your life! Female sportspeople in general – we've got such a high expectation [of them]. If we get passionate about something, we are 'hysterical' about it; if we get angry about something, we're 'losing control', whereas men can do whatever the hell they want. 'Oh yeah, he's very, very engaged in this.'

"I think it's great. It does affect your performance, having to hide who you are. You've got all that energy that goes into thinking about that instead. So imagine the freedom that they've got, that they can just be the sportsperson, and be fantastic at what they are."

There was, however, an inevitable darker side to the increased interest in women's football; for example, the vitriolic social media abuse some female players had found themselves subjected to.

"The things that come out of people's mouths, and you're just like, 'Are you serious?' When they're questioned, they don't know what you're talking about. They're so uneducated and ignorant.

"It makes me want to go and live on a mountain. [But] it has come on so much."

She reflected that when she was a teenager, she felt that being gay was something to be ashamed of, but her children simply could not comprehend that.

"[The children], they don't get it. But times move on, thankfully.

"I think the fact that players can now be openly who they are is just fantastic."

Farley appreciated the efforts that the FA were now making to recognise the contributions of the generations of female players prior to their rise to mainstream fame and celebrity, although she was at pains to say that she would not use the word 'grateful' simply for having the acknowledgement they deserved.

"You can either be bitter and twisted about it, or you can understand that you are part of that build-up to what has happened. I always think of the suffragettes, when they were fighting to get the vote and everything, and now you've got women that don't even bother voting. It's a period of time. It's a development, it's an evolving thing, and they could have easily just ignored us. They could have quite easily just gone, 'Yeah, let's not worry about the before,' but someone has gone and said, 'No, we need to recognise the people that went before.'"

She thought there was still room for improvement. With her two complimentary tickets for an England match, she had taken her daughter to Stadium MK in Milton Keynes, and realised that they were expected to queue for entry with the thousands who had paid for general admission. On taking their place in the line, she saw that the matchday programme had included a feature on her.

"I just looked at Poppy, and I went, 'I'm not doing this. I am not standing in this queue.'

"'What are you gonna do?'

"'We're going to the front and I'm going to tell them who I am.'

"'You can't do that!'

"'I've never done it before in my life, Poppy, but I'm going to do it.'

"And I walked to the front, and I said to one of the stewards at the front, 'Excuse me.'

"'Yes, yes, love?'

"'I'm not comfortable doing this,' I said, 'but that's me.'"

She brandished an imaginary programme. "'There's my ticket. Former player.'

"'Oh, my God, no, don't be ridiculous!' He was so lovely. He was like, 'No, you shouldn't have to stand in the queue! You get yourself in there!' And he let us in."

Farley had no regrets at all about her footballing career, and had no sense of wishing that she had been born two decades later and able to make the most of the financial investment and commercial opportunities that had come into the women's game after the turn of the millennium. She was endlessly entertained by people who knew that she had been a footballer and thus expected her to have made plenty of money from it, when in fact she was working another job throughout her time at the top, even at Hammarby.

"If we hadn't have done what we did, we've said this so many times, if we hadn't have dedicated our lives with no return…"

She paused and grinned. "We've got nothing out of it. I remember when Erica and I bought our first house where we live now, and we were new to the village, we didn't know anyone. Obviously I've made friends since, and found out that the rumour that went round the village was that I was an ex-professional footballer, and we bought the house [with] cash. Honestly, we sat around one evening, with friends, and everyone was having a few drinks, and they're like: 'So Karen, yeah, made a bit of money, didn't you?'

"'Doing what?'

"'With your football?'

"'No! Not a penny!'

"'Well, how did you buy the house cash then? That's the rumour that's gone around the village.'

The idea of being able to buy a house outright from monetary savings made solely from playing football was hilarious to her, a woman who had played at the Women's World Cup and won domestic trophies in Sweden and England. Nonetheless, she had no rancour about the delayed recognition for the achievements of her generation.

"I'm very much one of the ones that..." She stopped.

"I am very – " She stopped again. "I was almost going to say grateful, then. And I'm not grateful, I'm thankful that they've done it, because they could have easily not have done it. And why would I not want to be part of that? I think it's really important. I love history anyway, so we are part of history.

"I remember chatting to [England's Euro-winning captain] Leah Williamson once, and she was so lovely, and she said, 'You all keep saying it's so nice to meet us, but it's so cool for us to meet you guys, because without you lot, we wouldn't have what we have now, we wouldn't be able to do what we do now.'

"Bitterness, where's that going to get you? Yeah, not going to get you anywhere."

Although her place in English football history was only just being recognised, she had long held legendary status in Sweden. In 1994, she scored against Gideonsberg as Hammarby won their first-ever Swedish Cup, emerging triumphant in the final by two goals to one. Farley had celebrated her goal in inimitable style, flying forward with arms outstretched, hair flowing back from her headband, looking for all the world as if her delight might propel her to take off. The image had become iconic; when she turned fifty, the club's official social media account used it to illustrate their message of best wishes. It was also a photo that the team's supporters held near and dear to their hearts, using a much-enlarged version for a tifo – a fan-created art display in the stands, with individuals holding a piece above their heads to create the whole. Farley knew the tifo was going to be unveiled at one particular match in 2023, but was unable to attend due to a family holiday; however, her friends who were at the match kept her informed.

"My phone was like, ping, ping, ping, ping, ping!" she remembered.

"I wish I'd been there. It's magical. For them to sort of…"
She trailed off, obviously trying to count up the number of years it had been between her scoring that goal and the fan art, and in one way clearly amazed that they remembered it.

"It was like, twenty-nine, thirty years ago, and the people that had done it, they contacted me afterwards and said, 'I hope you saw it,' and they sent a picture.

"'That's amazing. Can I get a copy of the photograph?'

"'Absolutely, we will get one framed up for you and everything.'"

Farley was visiting Sweden a few weeks afterwards, and went to meet the fans in person. They had framed the photo with an inscription, and when she brought it home, she hung it on the wall of her cabin in the garden, dedicated to her trophies and other footballing memorabilia. Her beloved nephew Conor was impressed when he came to stay at Christmas. He had been a small child when she had been in her footballing prime, and had never quite grasped the impact his aunt had had on her clubs.

"He kept looking at it, and he said, 'That is so cool. I can't believe it, That is such a cool picture. I can't believe that's you. It really is. It's so awesome.'"

Conor and his partner Mary were about to return to their home in Sydney, Australia, where they had moved earlier that year as they sought to live out all their dreams after his cancer diagnosis. The night before they left, Farley secretly wrapped up the framed photo and put it in his suitcase as a gift and as a memento.

In 2021, Conor had been diagnosed with stage four stomach cancer, with an estimated eight weeks to live, but in autumn 2023 had been told that his body was showing no signs of active cancer cells. Six months later, his health took a turn for the worse, with the cancer entering his lymphatic system, and in April 2024 Farley and Conor's mother De flew out to Australia to be with him. He died at the age of thirty-one on Monday 13th May 2024.

As they packed up his belongings in the Sydney flat, Farley and Mary agreed that the treasured photo should go back to England and return to the wall of the cabin, a treasured memento of a fine career and now wreathed in additional memories of Conor.

"Women's football is such a safe space for everybody," reflected Farley. "I don't think I would take my children to men's football – I know I wouldn't, because they're just this air of aggression, whereas when you go to a women's [match], everyone's just happy. There's families, there's kids, there's mums, there's dads, there's everything, and it's just a really safe space."

She was less than impressed by the move towards segregating crowds, separating fans of opposing teams, which had been discussed at international level but had not been considered in women's football previously. Fans had traditionally been integrated, and in grounds with terracing some had even moved round the ground at half-time to stand behind the other goal in the second half.

"The only reason you have segregation is to stop people fighting, and for that herd [mentality], that allegiance kind of thing, but you don't need that in women's football," she said.

"It's just fun, it's just lovely. It doesn't matter if you're sat next to someone that supports the other team, because at the end of the day it's just a football match. No one's going to live or die."

WANDERER

In the beautiful Yorkshire village of Hebden Bridge during the 1980s, there were views aplenty, but opportunities few, at least for those girls with sporting ambitions. Isobel – Issy – Pollard did not come from a sporty background, but with a ball at her feet she felt absolutely at home, with no idea where the talent might have stemmed from. Her grandfather had played a little, her father played bowls and her mother had no interest in sport at all.

"I have no idea how I was naturally good at it," she said, "but I remember I used to drag my dad everywhere. I lived on a farm, if you will, and I just used to drag him down, my dad, down in the fields. I wanted to play in goal, I wanted to play anywhere, and I just dragged him to play football with me.

"I played at school. My headmaster back then, I remember my mum phoning him up to see if I could play in the team, and I can see that picture now: I was having lunch at school and he came and just sat down at the side of me and he said, 'Of course you can play in the team.' So I did that."

With the FA still taking a hands-off approach with women's football, the Women's FA were running the competitions. Pollard's mother contacted secretary Linda Whitehead to ask where the nearest women's team was, and discovered it was Bradford City, a roughly thirty-mile round trip from their home. Wanting to support their daughter's interest, they agreed to take her to training and matches three times a week, along with her commitments to hockey at a county level and her hobby of karate.

"I think my dad had to just give up bowling because he was like my chauffeur, to encourage me to do everything: karate twice a week, football twice a week, hockey once a week, hockey [match] on a Saturday, football [match] on a Sunday, and that's what happened for years."

Pollard spent around five years at Bradford City. There were no junior sides; she was straight into the action against grown women, having only experienced school football and kickarounds in the park with boys previously. Then she took a step up in the division and joined Bronte, a well-known independent name in the north, with famous names such as England's Clare Taylor representing them. Indeed, it was Taylor who had a huge impact on the direction of Pollard's footballing career at a very early point; with a limited coaching staff, the England manager did not have enough people to send out scouting across the country, so recommendations from established senior players were valued highly. At England camp, the coach mentioned that they were in need of a centre half to join up with the squad. Taylor suggested her sixteen-year-old Bronte team-mate.

Joining the squad was an overwhelming experience.

"I'd seen all these players growing up and obviously knew Clare, so I probably clung on to Clare a little bit for support," she admits. During that first England camp, there was a fun fair nearby, and some of the players happily went off to enjoy some of the rides. Pollard remembered waltzers in particular, and what she described as "this thing – you all sat around and it bounced up and down and then tipped on its side and it was just trying to bounce you off everything!"

It was unlikely that any of the other fair visitors recognised that they had the England squad among them – even if they were wearing what Pollard recalled as "these big stupid track-suits that didn't fit us". It was one of the few perks of the lack of investment and attention paid to women's football at the time, even at the elite level. Pollard's pal and Bronte team-mate Sammy Britton was often with her at England camp, and with the other younger players in the squad, they could be, by their own admission, "a little bit wild".

"We were going out clubbing, I think, after [a match]! Just what?! They can't do that now because they're so famous, aren't they? The paparazzi would just be following them everywhere.

"Obviously we're…"

Pollard paused.

"It wasn't big, was it? I mean, if you were in women's foot-ball back then, you knew who your players were. But yeah, you could probably get away with doing anything back then!"

Clare Taylor remembered that trip to the fun fair, and the team tracksuits they all wore. The defender also remembered the bruises they picked up from some of the more adrenaline-fuelled rides, which puzzled the physiotherapist treating them to prepare them for their matches.

"Those were the good old days," she said with more than a hint of humour. "Everyone thinks the era that they played in was good. Today's just totally different.

"Part of the fun for us was you've got another job to do and it just taught you real good time management. If you wanted to get to training, you've got to do this. With no mobile phones, you couldn't ring anyone and say, 'Oh yeah, I'm running a bit late,' or make excuses. You had to get there."

Although Taylor could not remember specifically giving the England coaches a nudge about Issy Pollard, that was certainly the way the system operated; they relied on the knowledge of their experienced players, and the quality control of top clubs such as Bronte and Doncaster Belles.

"They were always saying, 'Is there anybody?' because at the time, they weren't sending scouts, no, not at all. So it was more a case of 'If you know of anyone, just put names out there' – names into the hat!

"I remember Issy coming along [to England camp], with this ginger hair. She's a quiet character, but you could tell she'd got that killer instinct, very competitive. She was only about fifteen, something like that, [but] you can just tell, if they've got something about them.

"She'd got skill. She was really tenacious – not dirty. She was like a little fly where you just want to... 'Get out of my way!'"

Her overlap with Pollard at club level was limited; as the domestic women's game restructured towards a National League, Taylor opted to head west and join Knowsley, later to become Liverpool, managed by her old pal Liz Deighan.

Taylor was an experienced player by this point, and unlike her younger team-mate, had no wish to explore the option of pursuing a career overseas. She was more than happy with her day job at the post office, but she also played another sport at elite international level, becoming the first woman to play cricket and football at a World Cup. She won the cricket World Cup with England in 1993, and was part of the first England squad to go to a football Women's World Cup in 1995.

"I did get to a stage where one [sport] had to give, and the football gave over the cricket. I've been at the [football] World Cup '95, and then straight from there, we'd got a seven-week [cricket] tour to India. Obviously I missed some England [football] games there. Mo Marley came in, took my place, and then I just never got back in the England [football] team at all, and then the cricket just went from strength to strength. It was quite nice that England football wasn't working out. I just played England cricket."

Having said that, had she been given the choice, she may have opted for football over cricket.

"Hindsight is a great thing. Obviously, I'd got the longevity of the cricket career, but I think if you pushed me, I prefer football to cricket. At least in football, your destiny is in your own hands. As a centre half, if you give a penalty away, as long as it's not the 94th minute, you've got chance to go up from a corner [and get a goal back]. Cricket, once you're out, you're out. If you drop a catch, or you bowl a wide ball, you can't get it back. Cricket was more frustrating. That's more played from the neck up."

Had she had the opportunity to extend her football career, she was unsure whether she would have liked the rigours of playing professionally.

"It might be quite nice to give it a go, but in my own head, I was happy to be a postie and working out there, and putting some extra overtime into your mortgage, and then finding time then to go off and train. I used to pay a guy ten quid to do last two hours of my shift so I could get to Liverpool and go and play. That was just all part and parcel of it, and you accepted it was. That's how it was, and just got on with it."

⚽

In one of her first England matches, against Italy in October 1992, Pollard was named as substitute, but was used early on due to injury. Regular starter Jackie Sherrard was hurt not long after kick-off, meaning Pollard was called into action, and expected to mark one of the most dangerous players in the world – Carolina Morace.

"I was having palpitations! 'No! No!'" she laughed. "It was in Naples, only it was Avellino, so it's only a small stadium but still got flares and heaps of people there. So I was on. There was me as a sixteen-year-old and Sammy Britton, who was only barely eighteen, at the heart of the England defence, and that's all I'm thinking – against one of the most prolific centre forwards in European football Carolina Morace."

England were 2–0 down and Pollard was not surprised to get a scolding from the coaching staff, led by John Bilton, at half-time.

"I was like, 'Oh God, this is like big time, this!' But I kind of liked it. Chris Beaumont, who was my manager at Bronte, he was a bit of a hardcase, he was more of a shouter. So I was used to it, but I just thought, 'God, that's a bit of a wake-up call at England!'"

She added: "He were probably right [to shout]. I was shy, but playing with the big girls is a step up! It was a big thing. Looking back, especially like years after, when I look back, I think, 'Jesus Christ, they would never, ever now have a sixteen- and a seventeen-year-old at the heart [of defence], because there was no [talent] pathways, none.

"The kids are protected now, and they're guided from twelve, thirteen years old in the RTCs [regional talent centres], then they're into the PGAs [professional game academies], and then they're going into England, under-16s, under-19s, under-23s or whatever they do, and then they're rounded enough and they're conditioned enough to then step into senior, whereas we were straight in at sixteen, not protected.

"It's crazy, isn't it? We didn't know any different then. You just kind of got on with it."

After becoming a regular part of the England squad, she got to know the players based in the London area a bit better. Millwall Lionesses and Arsenal were dominating the game, and moving south seemed a perfect move for an ambitious teenager. It certainly made sense football-wise, but Pollard had never lived away from home before, and definitely not in London.

"Mum and Dad were disgusted that I made that decision to just dump all my studies," she grinned, "but I just wanted to follow my dreams, and I just thought, 'I'm just going to do it. I'm just going to get out of the valley and live in London for a couple of years,' which I did."

Pollard joined Millwall Lionesses, who looked after her very carefully. She stayed with fellow player Deb Bowring, and another new team-mate Dawn Willis got her a full-time job in the gym of a hotel on the Isle of Dogs. Even so, and with a club that ran in a much more professional way, training was still only twice a week, with match day on Sunday.

Sweden were taking their football much more seriously. Betsele coach Richard Holmlund came over to watch the English league, and invited Pollard to join his team.

"It was cold there in Betsele. It was near Lycksele, so I flew to Stockholm, and then we had to get a charter and then we had a two-hour drive north, so it was a really, really long way north, but oh my God, it was amazing. Eighteen, nineteen years old, just experiencing European football.

"And they've always been good, I think the Scandinavians were better then than they are now. The Danes, and Norway, and Sweden have always been good. It was just a brilliant, brilliant opportunity."

It was not the carefully organised transfer that any player would expect today when asked to move countries.

"Cor, dear," Pollard sighed. "Obviously they must have gone through Millwall, and Richard came out and watched. You think how it would work now; it would be so much more meticulously planned, discuss contracts and even a transfer fee. No, there was nothing like that. It was like, 'Do you want to come out to Sweden?'

"'Yeah, that would be great.'

"'When can you come out?'

"'This date.'

"'Great!'

"Pre-season, and then straight into the season, that was it. So there was no planning. They paid for the flights, I remember that. We got an apartment, and I've got a feeling we might have got fifty quid a week, possibly."

Arriving in the Swedish summer, it took time for Pollard to adjust to the near-full day of light, and coming from London to a quiet village with few facilities save a café that provided the players with their meals, despite a limited menu on offer, which got dull quickly. She was grateful, though, for all the attention the club paid to their players, including training three or four times a week, always in the late afternoon or early evening as the Swedish players were all at work during the day, and the provision of a match kit as well as training gear; in the mid-1990s, she recalled wryly, the three-quarter length cut was "really funky".

The pitches, however, were not what she was used to.

"It was so far north it was still snowing. When we went out, the lakes were still frozen.

"I remember the first game. When I used to play hockey we used to play on something called Redgra, it was a muddy gravel sort of thing. The pitch that we played our first game on, it was on this gravel."

Pollard and another of her new team-mates who had travelled over with her both scored in a 3–2 defeat.

"I jumped up. I think the ball hit me rather than me heading it, but it went in, because I remember the balls being so hard out there and I nearly fell unconscious after this header had gone in. It was an amazing goal. It must have looked fantastic!"

She stayed in Betsele for only a few months, which was always her plan.

"I liked the game in England," she said. "I think maybe if I'd have been at a First Division team [in Sweden] possibly [I would have stayed]. And the money, it wasn't enough, it weren't sustainable to stay out there for any big length of time."

She acknowledged that other players made their lives in their new country and never considered a return, making particular mention of her England team-mate Karen Farley's spell at Hammarby.

"It might have been a bit too early for me. If I'd have waited sort of like five or six years, potentially; if I'd have been twenty-four, twenty-five, going out there I think it might have been different. But when you get an opportunity, I didn't want to turn it down in case I didn't have the opportunity later in life. But yeah, I think it was probably before my time going as an eighteen, nineteen-year-old."

She was quick to say how welcoming her Betsele team-mates had been, and she was especially effusive about the coach Richard Holmlund. She had wanted to get back in touch with him but discovered he had passed away some years previously.

"He was a very, very good coach, was Richard Holmlund. He went to [top Swedish side] Umeå after us. I tried to track him down and he got killed in a road accident. He was going to be one of the [world's] top coaches; he had definitely coached in the first division – I think we were second division pushing [for promotion]. That's why he must have had the funding to be able to bring in a couple of international players. He was one of the best coaches around."

Pollard pointed out that men like Holmlund – and those before him – were pushing hard for women's football before there was much attention paid to it, and certainly before there was much financial investment.

"People in them day, the fellas, they were so far ahead of the game. I've got so much respect for the fellas, particularly in them days, that were really making a really big effort to try and change the pathway of women's football. They were still fighting. No one's fighting against it any more. I've got a lot of time for the fellas who put themselves out, because I can't imagine them getting paid much."

After a brief return to her former club Bronte, Pollard

signed for the legendary Doncaster Belles, which she had always dreamed of doing.

"I'd always wanted to join the Belles because they were just prolific, weren't they? And they set such a huge benchmark for decades. Playing with internationals, week in, week out, training with them – I probably regret not staying another season."

The ability and experience of the likes of Karen Walker and Pauline Cope inspired Pollard, and she moved on to Leeds United after a year.

"They were trying to build a squad, so I was one of the first ones to go to Leeds as they were developing it. So I spent about seven years there. Lucy Ward [now a TV co-commentator] came, Sue Smith [the former England international]. [Women's football] just got bigger and bigger and then they slipped away, didn't they, probably a few years back, did Leeds, which was a bit of a shame, because they were doing really well. It was brilliant. I met so many amazing people."

Pollard decided to retire from playing when she noticed herself slowing down and not being able to reach the standards she had set herself, although she had still joined in an occasional training session at Everton with her old team-mate Sammy Britton, and wondered whether she should have carried on for at least another year.

As the game began its current boom, and the new generation of Lionesses enjoyed such success under the management of Sarina Wiegman, the renewed interest in those who had played for England in previous years had shone a spotlight on Pollard and her generation, which she found strange in some ways but also invigorating. She had also got back in regular contact with some of the women who had been her close friends during her playing career; indeed, she was even working alongside one of her best pals from Millwall, Julie Fletcher, in a player management services role.

She speculated that she could have spent longer at Doncaster Belles, and wondered if she should have considered joining Arsenal, who she trained with a few times under the management of the legendary Vic Akers, a man with whom she got on very well, which would also have given her the chance to reunite with some of her friends from Bronte who left for London at the same time as she did. However, the one big regret of her playing career was not taking up the chance of a college scholarship to the USA, which she was offered prior to going to Sweden. A few years later, it became de rigueur for the ambitious female footballer to head to the States and enjoy competitive football while obtaining a tertiary degree, but when Pollard was approached, she would have been one of the very first from England to go.

"Kelly Smith was soon after me. Nobody was really doing it then. I can remember his name, Andy Bonchonsky at University of San Francisco, and I had a couple of calls with him, and he was desperate to get me over, because I think if you're at any international level, they just want you, even now.

"And I'm not quite sure why I didn't. Maybe it was the fear – a long way to go for four years, three or four years' commitment, so possibly the commitment thing. But then I've obviously seen how well Kelly did at Seton Hall and Rachel Brown at Alabama. Then you're thinking, 'Oh, God, that could have been me, one of the pioneers that did it.'

"It weren't to be, but yep, big regret. If I were to have my time again, I would take it."

She added: "The America thing would have been life-changing for me, definitely, because the game out there was big then. It has always been big – hasn't it? – but it was big then because it was Mia Hamm, Brandi Chastain, Michelle Akers-Stahl – they were the [top USA] players at that time. It was phenomenal."

Pollard did go to the USA, though, as she embarked on her coaching career, spending several months out there and staying with host families.

"I've gone from Hebden Bridge to London, London to Sweden, Sweden to UK, UK to America," she listed out, adding that her parents wondered where she might decide to move next. Indeed, she admitted she may have gone to even more countries to play had the chance arisen.

"It wasn't as easy as it is now, because [coaches] can tap onto Wyscout [an online scouting platform] and just see your players and you can just scout. I'm doing some scouting at the moment and I know you're getting watched all the time. As soon as you step foot on the pitch, there's somebody watching you, whether it's from a video, or whether it's someone with a hood up somewhere. It's pressure, there's a lot of pressure on the kids now to keep performing."

This knowledge from the inside of the game helped her to

develop her own philosophy of working with young players, supporting them to make the right choices for their own careers.

Again, her own international background gave her credibility.

"When I put in a LinkedIn connection or if I've dropped somebody a message, I know they've been to look at my page to make sure that I'm not an… arse," she laughed, having paused to seek out the right word and plumping for the colloquial. "So they look at my page and they're like, 'Oh, yeah, she's all right,' and I get a connection straight away, or get a reply, or I get a response.

"People listen to me and I can speak to anybody in any academy. Agents are frowned upon, and they've not got a good name in men's football, let alone in women's football. We just want to make that a little bit different.

"We're looking after our athletes, we're talking to them. We phone in every three or four weeks to make sure they're all right, and I bet not many agents do that."

She had taken the decision to step away from coaching, feeling she did not have the right passion for it, and instead found a different way to be involved in the game, taking scouting and talent identification courses. She had not been impressed at the way some of the soccer scholarship firms operated, and wanted to make sure that young female talent was being advised and cared for by people who had specific knowledge of the women's game. A woman working with a female player, she thought, had a greater insight and greater confidence when it came to broaching conversations on both sides, whether that was about the right kind of sports bras or menstrual or gynaecological problems.

"As a male agent, that would be difficult to speak to players about bouncy boobs, whereas we have a chat with our girls and say, 'Do you fancy trying [these bras] out, see what they're like?'

"And we can have them personal conversations about periods. If they're not feeling that great [and thinking], 'How do I tell my manager this, that and the other?' then they can reach out to me and Julie, and I love that part of it. It's so nice, with the pressures that they're under now as well."

As a trade-off, though, the pressure that elite young female players were facing also went hand in hand with increased money, visibility, facilities, opportunities and more. Pollard was delighted to see the way the women's game had progressed globally even in the short time since she had hung up her own boots. She was also pleased to see some of the recognition that was being given to previous generations of England players – even those who had played unofficially. The so-called 'Lost Lionesses', who had represented Britain at the unsanctioned invitational Women's World Cup in 1971, had featured in a critically well-received feature film documentary, called *Copa 71*, with backing from American soccer legends such as Brandi Chastain and sporting icons Venus and Serena Williams. Pollard was glad their story was being told, as well as those who had played for England in later years.

"I know they weren't the real England squad, if you will,"

she said. "They were a squad that was put together by a man [Harry Batt] who was way before his time, wanting to allow girls to play football. And they were banned from everywhere."

The efforts the football authorities were making now to redress the indignities and disparities that female footballers had faced previously were welcome, of course, but, Pollard thought, the least that could be done.

"I mean, it's great. I think it's amazing. We wouldn't be where we are now had they not put in the effort in terms of the strategies and everything they've got, regarding the pathways, ETCs [Emerging Talent Centres] and the PGAs [Professional Game Academy]. It's phenomenal what they've done.

"I think it's brilliant what they're doing for the young girls, especially the opportunities now. Unbelievable."

"Girls can't play football."

Samantha Britton – better known as Sammy – was convinced that she was the only girl who enjoyed kicking a ball around. Born in 1973, she joined in with the boys' games at junior school, and even when she moved to high school and was not officially allowed to play with them any longer, she was still part of the matches at break time, along with her best friend Helen. Despite not officially being permitted to participate, Britton was even part of a school football trip to a tournament in Malta, which was the first time she ever played a formal match.

Barry Daly, the manager of Huddersfield Ladies, was working at Britton's school, and spotted her talent. He was desperate for her to join his team, but fifteen-year-old Britton was unconvinced that any women's team might be good. So he tried a different approach.

"He said to me one day, 'Can you come, even if it's just once, and show them some of your skills?' And then I went, and that were it. I just kept going."

Daly knew that Britton had what it took to reach the very top of the women's game, even if she herself had no idea of the possible pathway.

"He was saying, 'You could play for England!' and I was saying, and I said, 'What England?'

"I didn't even know there was an England team! 'What do you mean, England?' And he's like, 'Yeah, there's an England team.' I didn't even know. It was weird. To not know there was an England team, and you like football – it's just strange, in't it?"

Still, even though she had been talked into joining Huddersfield, that did not mean she was overly impressed with the standard of play she saw. Because she had been so used to playing alongside and against boys of her own age, she was used to a bigger physical challenge, despite being the youngest in the women's squad. She shone immediately, slotting into any outfield position where she might be required, and her undoubted ability combined with her invaluable versatility meant she was called up to the England under-21 squad within a year, joining the senior team in 1992, still under the auspices of the Women's FA rather than the FA proper. Britton described the set-up as lacking professionalism – unsurprisingly with an organisation dependent on volunteer labour. With players covering most of their own costs, and crowds very limited with so little publicity, it was no wonder that Britton's memory of her early England days was: "They had nothing to offer you."

Britton's family were not big football fans, and she was never the kind of person to talk about her sporting achievements, so her footballing career continued almost under a veil of silence – even internationally.

"For some of them, playing for England were the be-all and end-all. But for me, it were just another game," she explained, then added: "It was still good. Don't get me wrong, you're proud and you're representing your country and you're playing against the top teams and top players. But at the same time, it was just no big [thing] for me, it was just my hobby."

It was a hobby that took her across the world, notably to Sweden in 1995 as part of the first England squad to compete in a FIFA Women's World Cup. Despite the big occasion, Britton found it quite gruelling, not least because she was not used to being away from home.

"That was the first tournament football I'd played. Before, you'd maybe go away for four or five days if you were playing a team, tops, and all of a sudden you're away for three weeks.

"It was enjoyable, but at the same time, it was, 'I just want to get home.' But you're in a World Cup. Mixed emotions, really, you're playing in a World Cup, but the same time you're trying to deal with [it being] the first time you've been away from home for so long with these people."

On arrival, Britton had been impressed with the spectacle of the tournament's opening ceremony, and the size of the crowd for Sweden's first match, against Brazil in Helsingborg – 14,500 the official attendance. In the same stadium the next day, England played their opening match against Canada, in front of just 655 fans.

"The opening ceremony was quite big, and it was like, 'Wow, that was good.' They put on a little show, and the crowd was quite big. The game followed, the crowd noise and the atmosphere was great, I couldn't wait to get started, and it was big, and [they were] cheering, and then we played Canada a few days later, and it was like, 'Wait, what's happened? There's no one here.'

"I was excited to play in that atmosphere of the opening ceremony and it didn't happen. It was just really strange. I've been watching women's matches recently, the contrast is unbelievable. To play for England is absolutely huge now. Your life is set, everything, whereas to play for England when I was young was nothing."

When the squad returned from the World Cup, eliminated in the quarter-finals by Germany, they arrived back in England wearing their standard-issue uniform – skirts and blazers. This was hardly Britton's style.

"I'm like, 'I can't believe they've made me wear a skirt, bearing in mind I've not worn a skirt since I was about ten.' When I wore a skirt to play netball at school, I had tracksuit bottoms. I just didn't wear skirts. A lot of us weren't comfortable in them."

By that time, Britton had joined Arsenal Ladies. After deciding to leave the Gunners, she was contacted by Cove Rangers in Scotland, where a former team-mate was playing. They offered her a car and expenses, and told her that she did not need to train, just to turn up for matches on a Sunday. She lived in Glasgow and travelled to Aberdeen for home games – a roughly 300-mile round trip. The travel time did not seem to hamper her as she helped her new team to lift the Women's Scottish Cup, notching a hat-trick in the semi-final against Giuliano's in 1997.

Her success obviously caught the attention of the England selectors, who got in touch with her and, after learning that she did not perceive herself to be ready for international action and was not training regularly, asked her to get herself fit because they wanted her back in the squad.

"I just thought, 'Sod you lot,'" admitted Britton, who did not step up her training and did not intend to return to the international fold. After more phone conversations, she changed her mind, and also left Scotland, joining Croydon, and then Doncaster Belles, before signing for Everton. A chance encounter during a friendly match there against Icelandic side IBV gave her an unexpected opportunity, when their coach Heimir Hallgrímsson asked her if she would be interested in joining them. Because they competed domestically in a summer season, it would not clash with representing Everton. More importantly, for the very first time she would be paid a wage for playing football.

"It wasn't even [mainland] Iceland. It's called Vestmannaeyjar, it's a small island off of Iceland, and it's literally three square miles, and that is it. It's basically got a little tiny bit where the houses are, and it's just surrounded by volcanic rocks and beautiful scenery.

"Honestly, there's nothing, nothing there. I got there, and I thought, 'I'm going to need to go home. I can't stay here,' because my life was hectic. I was non-stop. I was here, I was there, and I've gone to this island.

"Look out of your window for two hours, you don't see one person. It's just like, 'Where am I? I can't live here.' That's what I was thinking. Someone said, 'We'll take you to town.' We went to two shops and we went to a café. I said, 'When are we going to town?' and they said, 'We've just been.'

"I'm not a drinker, but there was one pub on the island, which opened on a Tuesday and a Thursday or something. The hospital was closed, but if you got hurt, they opened up the hospital for you. It's just crazy, but beautiful, one of the most beautiful and innocent places I've ever been, if I'm honest.

"So after about a week, I could feel myself..." She paused, and exhaled heavily to indicate the dissipation of stress and anxiety. "'This is actually all right, my phone's not going and this ain't going.' The training, healthy lifestyle, the food, the amazing people, it just worked for me. And obviously I was getting money, so that helped as well."

Britton spent one full season out there, plus a few weeks across two other summers, enabling her to get fully sharp ahead of the English season, and in her final year there to benefit from some rehab after snapping her cruciate ligament; indeed, she was fit enough to play the second half of the season and help IBV to their first-ever Icelandic Cup in 2004. However, her tense and problematic relationship with the England set-up continued when, towards the end of the year 2000 and during the qualification campaign for the following year's European Championships, she pre-empted a possible positive drugs test by telling the authorities that she had smoked marijuana.

She is now at pains to say that she hopes what she says about her memory of the incident does not give the impression that she condones any form of drug-taking, including alcohol, regardless of whether it is for recreational use. She was called in front of an FA panel convened at Lilleshall, who seemed amazed that she was openly and honestly speaking about her marijuana use.

"I said, 'I've got nothing to hide. Something's happened in my life, and I felt, instead of going to the doctor and waiting six weeks for antidepressants to kick in, I did what I know works for me, and I smoked a spliff. What do you want me to say?'

"They were shocked that I just come straight out and said it, and I didn't just say it, I had an argument for it."

She was convinced she had a point, adding that it was not a performance-enhancing drug, but did accept that there were rules in place that she had broken and that there would be consequences. The authorities were looking to hand out a suspension from international football to Britton as well as a period of rehabilitation, telling her she would have to be admitted for a month, which she refused to do due to starting a new job. She recalled that the expert who initially assessed her reported back that she did not have a drug problem, as it was clear that she would go months without smoking at all. After that, an on-field disciplinary offence from a decade earlier was mentioned as a reason for her to require treatment; this suggestion that she would benefit from anger management made her laugh, as they were referring to a red card ten years previously, and she had not been sent off again in the years since, picking up very few yellow cards. Ultimately, she accepted her punishment, knowing that she would need to do so if she wanted to play for England again, and agreed to go for one week. Indeed, when she found out how much a month of rehab would cost, she sarcastically suggested that perhaps they could pay her directly and she would promise she would never do it again.

"I was angry about that, because I didn't want to go. Just didn't want to go. Didn't think there was a reason," she said.

"I went for a week and, I tell you what, it taught me a lot."

The techniques of personal reflection and development were, she thought, useful, but the group meetings that she was encouraged to attend were not.

"The first day I got there, getting everyone to stand up to say, 'My name is so and so, and I'm an alcoholic.' I said,

'What am I supposed to say?'" The majority of the group were there because of alcohol, and Britton learnt a lot about their experiences and the struggles of others with addiction and mental health issues. She met people who had lost everything – family, children, houses, jobs – and were now going through the toughest battle of their lives, and saw first-hand that addictions did not discriminate. She felt fortunate; she had not lost anything or hurt anyone, and her life was great apart from the inconvenience of being in rehab.

"I said, 'I'm never going to one of them meetings again,' and they didn't make me. I'm not standing up and saying something I don't believe so it was very interesting, and I'm kind of glad I went, but at the same time, it was taking the mickey! [In my eyes] I hadn't done owt."

Britton was in rehab only because she wanted to play for England again; she chose football, showing her just how important it was to her.

"Obviously I enjoyed playing football, although I didn't enjoy all parts of it. Whether they called me back [into the England squad] or not, it was important to me, but I felt my life wouldn't have changed that much if they didn't."

She loved the friends she had made through football, and treasured the memories the game had given her, but it was not an obsession.

"Some people eat, sleep, drink football. I don't. I never have. I play and I go home. I don't think about it. I don't watch it. I didn't use to hardly train, and people used to say, 'Oh, my

God, I can't believe you!' I'd say, 'Yeah, but we're not getting paid. I've got other things going on my life. I don't have time. I'm working full-time. I've got friends, a partner, I've got a family, other hobbies. I just don't have time.'

"I work from Monday to Friday, and then Friday, I drive to Everton, train, come back on a Friday night at 11 o'clock. Then maybe wake up on the Saturday, go back to Liverpool, then get taken to London to play, for example, Arsenal. Stay there on the Saturday. Play on the Sunday, come back Sunday evening to Liverpool, get back in my car to Huddersfield. So I'm getting back at could be 10 o'clock, and then go to work Monday morning."

Britton did return to the Everton and England folds, later signing for Leeds United for two years before going back to the blue side of Merseyside. Her last England call-up came in May 2005, when she was an unused substitute against Norway. The number of caps she gathered is unclear, with line-ups not recorded accurately during the early part of her career, but women's football historian Professor Jean Williams once estimated that Britton made 67 full appearances. It is possible that this is an underestimate.

Yet Britton still had not received her legacy cap from the FA, recognising her contributions as the 88th player selected to represent the England team. She had not been able to attend a match where there would be a formal presentation, but she wished that it could have been posted to her instead to save her the glare of the spotlight, which still made her uncomfortable. Although she was amazed at the growth of women's football and the instant celebrity of the top players, she was glad that she had been born early enough to evade those demands.

"When I was six or seven, if I had been in some academy, I think, 'Jesus Christ, what kind of a player [would I have been]?'

"I wouldn't have had the life I have if I'd have been playing now, but at the same time, I'd have been set for life. I [wouldn't] like the fame. I don't like interviews. I'm not that sort. I was captain once. I absolutely hated it because I had to do a press conference. I'm not into that side. So when I think about the game now, I say, 'Give me the money, but not the fame.'"

She considered. "But yeah, just the feeling of playing in front of such big crowds and every single player being fully fit, a real athlete. We had, like, three athletes in the whole England team, and everyone else were breathing out their arse – especially me! When you played for England you were like, 'Oh my God!' You worked to push yourself an extra gear, or two or three in my case, and we didn't have it. Technically, I don't think there's much difference; I think we had unbelievable technical players. But when you see the fitness and obviously they're doing it day in, day out, so it's drilled, the positioning, I think it's..."

She stopped herself. "I shouldn't be saying, 'It's amazing [now].' I think this is why I get mad, because it should have been like that from day dot.

"With time, a lot of fighting, a lot of determination, things have got so much better. Every girl has the opportunity to dream about football as a career, and she has female role models she can strive to be like.

"At least they've got it now."

PART THREE

Obviously the standard we play is far different to what they play. We've only got to learn from the Germans, the Swedes and Norwegians. We can only go from there really... We're still far behind.

Gillian Coultard, England player, 13th June 1995

LATECOMER

Pauline Cope spent a decade in England's number one shirt, winning sixty caps. She began her career with Millwall Lionesses, though she spent time at other London clubs including Arsenal and Croydon. A league winner, a cup winner, part of England's first-ever Women's World Cup squad, she was more than qualified to spot talent – and occasionally it presented itself in the most unexpected locations.

"I lived in a flat in Dartford, and it was three storeys. I'd just bought a flat on the top floor, and her mum just bought a flat on the ground floor. Her mum kept seeing me in my football kit, and we started chatting. I was saying I play football and she said, 'Oh, my daughter's into football. She's a runner, but she loves football.'

"I said, 'Invite her down to Millwall.' And lo and behold, Dan came down to Millwall, and as they say, the rest is history. She was a natural athlete anyway, being a runner, but to add being technically a good footballer in the mix, you've got the perfect footballer."

This chance meeting with the legendary Cope led to Danielle Murphy – better known to most simply as Dan – joining with the iconic Millwall Lionesses – one of the leading lights in domestic women's football during the late 1980s and early

1990s, they were entirely independent at first but then became loosely attached to the men's club who shared their name, giving them access to some of the professional facilities there as part of their community outreach programme.

Murphy was something of an odd mix – a prodigiously young talent who had yet come to the game comparatively late. Within two years of that first chat with Cope – when Murphy was just fourteen – the two were part of the same England squad, with Murphy making her England debut four years after Issy Pollard's final appearance on the bench as an unused substitute. Not only that, but making her first substitute appearance against Scotland on 23rd August 1997, at the age of sixteen years and two months, she was also the youngest debutant for the national team since it had fallen under the FA's remit. It was quite the achievement.

"My parents loved it. The school was really supportive. Everyone was really supportive."

Murphy adapted quickly to international duty, already used to playing senior football alongside women who were sometimes as much as twice her age.

"You'd go away, travel to all places as well, so you had to hold your own in that environment," she remembered. "Pauline Cope took me under her wing, basically. She was always a big supporter [of mine]. She was involved in England, and was a big personality, it helped if you were in with a big personality."

Many of her Millwall team-mates were also in the England squad, which helped her to settle in. The endorsement of

Millwall, though, did not mean that their resources were infinite.

"Katie Chapman was there, the Hunt twins [Carly and Gemma] were there, Copey was there, Mary Phillip was there," she listed. "We had a really good team, like a really good young team, and the training was really odd."

She gave the example of arriving at the Den and doing an hour of fitness training by running round the underground tunnels in the stadium, triggering the movement-activated lights as they sprinted past, before heading to the sports hall for their actual football training. They worked together as a squad twice a week, meaning that it was up to individuals to do extra work by themselves if they wanted to. Murphy was keen on fitness and endurance, and put those hours in.

"I did have that mentality," she said. "We were training with the facilities that we had and the time limits that we had, we were still putting in the work in, and then you're also competing, because at that time, it was quite competitive to get into that team as well, but you had limited time and limited facilities."

Murphy was combining all of this with her A-level study and university applications. She had been considering the institutions with good sporting reputations, such as Loughborough and Liverpool John Moores, until one day the phone rang.

"I answered the phone.

"'This is Becky Burleigh, at the University of Florida, and we're recruiting players. We've seen your name.'

"I was like, 'Dad, there's an American woman on the phone!'

"He went, 'Talk to her!'

"I went, 'Oh, yeah, OK, yeah!'"

Murphy's international caps had got her name known globally. Burleigh's University of Florida side had just won the national championship, and she was looking to recruit for the coming academic year. A senior international player would be a great asset to the squad. Burleigh and her assistant wanted to come and see Murphy in action in person.

"Millwall were playing against Croydon somewhere in, like, the deepest, darkest depths of Crystal Palace somewhere," recalled Murphy, "and they flew over on a Saturday morning or a Sunday morning, watched the game, and then flew back home the next day. It was the weirdest thing."

She grinned slightly shamefacedly. "I played rubbish as well, really rubbish!"

She thought her chance of going to America had dissolved, but Burleigh and her assistant travelled to the Murphy house in Sevenoaks, and sat down in the kitchen with Dan and her father.

"Vic [Campbell], the assistant coach, all I remember is him like eating a whole packet of Rich Tea biscuits, and he kept saying, 'We don't have these in America!'" she laughed.

"And then they said, 'Right, we really are interested.'"

They went through their scholarship offer, which covered a lot of Murphy's expected expenses, with her father asked to pay for accommodation and food.

"Then they were like, 'Do you want to come out and see it?'"
"I was like, 'What?!'"
"They said, 'Well, you can come out for a recruitment trip.'"
"English universities don't say, 'Come over. We'll pay for you to come and have a look!'"

Of course Murphy took up the invitation, going over for a weekend, landing at Orlando and met by a driver who took her to campus in Gainesville, two hours north. She got to meet her potential team-mates, and saw them play in front of many more spectators than she was used to seeing in England for women's games.

"At the game there was, I'd say, two or 3,000 people," she estimated. "Then you go along the campus and then there was a 90,000-seat stadium for American football, and then there was a 20,000-seat stadium for basketball.

"And then they were like, 'Do you want to come here?'"
"I was like, 'Uh-huh!'"

Although the Dick, Kerr Ladies toured the USA to much acclaim in the early part of the twentieth century, showing the appetite there could be for women's football, the real gamechanger that rocket-charged the women's game's development there was the 1972 introduction of the law known as Title IX, guaranteeing equal financial investment in men's and women's sport within educational settings. That meant that college sport – a huge national pastime in the USA – would now also give equal weight to its women's teams. Numbers of participants boomed; it was no wonder that it was an Olympic Games in America that first hosted women's football, in 1996, and that images from its 1999 Women's World Cup triumph had become iconic, most notably Brandi Chastain's famous celebration after scoring the winning penalty kick, tearing off her shirt and roaring as she slid along the pitch on her knees.

Florida Gators coach Becky Burleigh had heard about Murphy on the grapevine. A player that young with so much senior international experience was of interest to a US college team looking to improve its already impressive record. Burleigh remembered very well her trip to see Murphy play.

"It was crazy. I didn't even change [the time on] my watch."

She and her assistant flew in to the UK on Sunday morning, watched the Millwall Lionesses game, met with Murphy and her father, and then flew back to the States. In contrast to Murphy's memory that she had played badly, Burleigh immediately saw the qualities she wanted in her squad.

"As soon as I saw her play, I was like, 'Yep, we need her,'" she said.

"If you know Murph, I mean, that's one tough woman right there, and as soon as you see her and get to know her, first of all, she's very personable. I loved having her on our team. Second of all, she is just a warrior. So you have those two combination traits of her being such a tremendous team-mate, and her being such a great asset in terms of just the culture and work ethic and how tough she was."

Burleigh knew the excellent sporting facilities at the University of Florida would turn the head of any aspiring athlete; the space and the funding was way beyond the means of any individual football club in England. However, she also knew that spending four years in a different country was in no way an easy decision to make.

"You just never know about somebody coming that far and leaving their family and all that part of it," she said, "but Murph was one of a kind, so I'm not surprised she did. She's a pretty independent woman."

Burleigh had, as she described it, "a special place" in her heart for the international students who committed to Florida for their university study, moving to a different country and leaving their friends, family and built-in support network. That meant that when Murphy agreed to join, Burleigh was ready to look out particularly for her, to ensure that she was happy and settling in and enjoying her new life.

⚽

Just because Murphy was a much-admired footballer – or a Florida Gators' 'soccer player' as she was about to become in the US – it did not mean that she could neglect her academic studies. Even though she passed her A-levels, she also had to take the American SAT before she could be formally admitted, which gauged her verbal and mathematical reasoning. Not used to the American scholastic format, Murphy found that the paper "may as well have been in a foreign language", and was promptly put in to summer school to improve her attainment prior to the official start of pre-season. In retrospect, this was a footballing benefit to her as well, because it gave her the chance to adapt to a very different climate.

"If it was 70 degrees in the winter months of Florida, they were wearing a jumper. I was like, 'What is this?!'" she laughed.

"You had to pass a fitness test before you could even take part in pre-season, which was then three [training sessions] a day for two weeks, then the season started, and the season was only from August until Christmas time, so there was two games a week, but it was brilliant and really intense."

The intensity was something she loved right from the off. She had been used to doing her own additional fitness work at Millwall Lionesses; now she was training every day with the rest of the Gators squad team-mates with facilities she had never had encountered before. What was more, she thrived on it.

"I'd always been into the endurance and fitness side of the sport anyway," she said. "I felt like they kind of wanted an athlete, and then they could make them into a footballer. Over time, everything evolved, but the training sessions were really intense, but I loved it. I loved it. That's what I wanted. The running until someone gives up, or one person makes a mistake, it's the whole team.

"I remember we used to do walking lunges up and down the pitch as a punishment. One time, they made us roll up on our sides from one end all the way up to the end of the pitch, because we had obviously missed a shot or something. It's the weirdest thing.

"Then obviously the strength and conditioning was good; that brought the other side of my game as well, but the facilities were unbelievable."

Players in their first year in the American collegiate system rarely made it into the starting eleven, but Murphy did.

"I think I was one of their biggest surprises," she admitted, "because when they would put you on the line and say, 'Run and run and run and run and run,' I'd just do it, because I enjoyed it."

Murphy loved being a 'jock' – a sports student – and treated almost as a professional athlete, with her football much more important than her studies, although she knew she had to keep up her grades in order to stay as part of the squad. She opted to major in sociology, which she had studied at A-level.

"Looking back as an old lady," she reflected wryly, "well, maybe I could have gone into something I could possibly have used a little bit more, but at that point you're just training every day, travelling around the country, and wanting to maintain a GPA [grade point average] that allows you to play."

It was a lifestyle she certainly would not have got at a British university, and most definitely not in the domestic English league.

"You'd go into the locker room and you'd have your own facilities. It was all so well done. You were made to feel special, even your name on your jersey. You'd get all your kit sorted out for you.

"People on the campus knew that you was a jock. You were part of that community. All of the sports hung out together, we would socialise together.

"Even the training facilities were better than the pitches that you would play on here [in England] in games. We would fly to games. We would charter our own flights. You'd get a bus, you would drive to an airport, and then you'd get on the airplane, you'd be the only ones on there. It's the maddest thing."

Perhaps it was not surprising that Murphy – already a two-year veteran of the England national team – never looked back. There had been no tears at Gatwick airport as her parents saw her off with just her two bags of luggage going with her. She was used to being relatively independent, and enjoyed the freedom that college life gave her. What did become difficult to manage was the stress of balancing all her responsibilities: representing the university, keeping up her grades, and the travel and commitment required to be part of the England camp.

"You're the only one making decisions in your life," said Murphy of her first year at college. "You've got to make new friendships, you've got to make new relationships, you've got to have the motivation to get yourself to class. It was a big eye-opening thing. It helped that I was in the accommodation on the campus for the first year, so you got your own social circle there, and I never really felt that lost.

"The hardest thing was coming backwards and forwards playing for England, and trying to maintain that. I really did struggle with that at the time. It was probably towards the end of my first year, going into my second, I was just like, 'This is too exhausting.'"

With her father, Murphy wrote a letter to England coach – and her former Millwall team-mate – Hope Powell explaining that she needed to focus on her studies in the USA, adding that she would like to return to the international fold when she had graduated. She got no response to her note, and was never picked for England again.

"Here's the thing that we never know," reflected Gators coach Becky Burleigh. "Is it like, 'Out of sight, out of mind' for kids that come over [to the USA]? Is it like they want to stick to the kids who are domestic? And if so, that's a shame, because it feels like we can play a part in developing their game and giving them exposure to some things that they might not have."

It did, however, mean Murphy got to concentrate on representing the University of Florida and achieving her degree, and she valued the support of the coaching staff and her team-mates there, which she described as a "family". She was particularly complimentary of Burleigh, then relatively early on in her coaching career, but whose achievements subsequently were ground-breaking, including becoming one of only two women who had over 500 match wins in college competition.

"She's got something special about her," Murphy said of Burleigh, "a definite aura about her. One on one, she makes you feel good, and she was a parent to a lot of people at one time. And yes, she has to deal with all of the emotional side of that as well, which comes with putting twenty teenage girls in a room.

"I always had quite a special relationship with her, but I feel like there were many people who would say that about her. I was very lucky that she was in my life. She's cool as well, she's a cool person to be around.

"She's relatable. She didn't ever shy away from something. She was a talker. So there was never this, 'We're not going to confront this.' 'We are going to confront it, however hard it is,' and so that's what I liked. You knew where you stood with her."

Burleigh was equally complimentary of her player.

"I just loved Murph's personality. She lives large. She plays hard; honestly, she partied hard, but she was a giver. I just really loved having her as part of our team, because I thought she was very committed to the cause. I thought she was very committed to her teammates, and she's just a good person to be around. She's honest, hard-working. When you describe somebody that you want on your team like you're pretty much describing Murph."

Murphy graduated in 2003, but emerged into a very different world. The terrorist attacks on 11th September 2001 had heightened security and added necessary obstacles to international travel. Murphy had considered staying on to do a Master's degree, but the cross-Atlantic flights were now even more difficult, and she knew that getting a green card and having the right to live and work in the USA would be tough and a very long process. More than that, the Women's United Soccer Association (or WUSA), the top flight of women's domestic competition in the USA, was in the process of folding after three seasons of professional competition, closing in September 2003, so there were no clubs where she would immediately be able to pursue professional football.

"It's too bad, because she would have been great," said Burleigh. "She would have been great for this league."

Instead, Murphy headed back to England, signing for Charlton Athletic, and later for Watford.

"It was sad because I didn't want to leave, I would have stayed out there totally if I could have done," she said. "It's really weird, the direction that your life takes."

Murphy's decision to join Charlton Athletic on her return from the USA was inevitable. Her old friend Pauline Cope was there and she would not have countenanced any other choice. The two had stayed in touch since that very first day Murphy went to train with Millwall Lionesses, and Cope felt a certain amount of responsibility towards the younger woman. She agreed that she had taken Murphy under her wing at Millwall and during England camps.

"I was the one who encouraged her into coming down to Millwall, it was only right for me to protect her like a big sister.

"She didn't need much protecting. She could look after her own, Dan. But yeah, I looked out for her like I did with a lot of the kids, really."

She added: "I always had a soft spot for Dan, looking out for her and seeing her progress. I remember visiting her when she lived with her dad in Sevenoaks, when she was off to America, and I got quite emotional when I said to her, 'You look after yourself out there, and if it ain't right for you, you come straight back.' It was quite an emotional time. I felt like [I was] sending my little sister off to college."

Cope felt that the younger Murphy was inclined to keep herself to herself, and never confided in her about how she felt about the premature end of her England career.

"She's very private, yeah, and then she kept a lot to herself. I wouldn't use the word 'embarrassed', but she didn't want people to know her business, and she kept very things very close to her chest," Cope explained. "I tried to draw it out of her, but I'm not one to be pushy. People don't want to talk, I'm not going to be bang, bang, bang on at them. She knew I was there if she wanted someone to talk to, but she was very private, very private, and I respected that privacy."

Cope admired Murphy's courage in leaving her support network and starting a new life in the USA.

"I'm so much of a home person, I've never taken risks. I don't know whether it's because I've never had the support network to go, 'Go on, you can do it,' or whether I just haven't got that in me to take risks: if it doesn't work, how am I going to come back from that? Dan had that in abundance. She had a lot of people supporting her. I suppose being young, she never had any responsibilities, a mortgage, kids, she was like a free spirit, really. If you're that young and you've got no ties, why not give it a go? If it doesn't work, you come back. It's that simple.

"And she took a chance, she took that gamble, and, yeah, she did love it out there."

⚽

A few years later, Murphy successfully applied for the assistant manager's role at Arkansas, but ultimately turned it down as she had achieved one of her other career ambitions – entering the fire service, where she had been ever since.

"I love it," she said. "It's brilliant. I love it. It gives me that family, camaraderie, team thing every day. So that's what I need."

After hanging up her football boots, she had played hockey for a local team for a while before having her family, and did not speculate on what footballing heights she might have reached had she been born just a couple of years later: able to graduate from Florida and then immediately join a team in the USA's new professional league, Women's Professional Soccer (WPS), which began in 2009; or perhaps later to head back to England and become part of the first-ever Women's Super League season in 2011. She was thrilled to see the current generation of England players not only play professional football but to become mainstream celebrities.

"I'm the biggest fan," she said. "You go. You go, girls! I love where it's gone. I love that people now know their names. Brilliant.

"Young girls who don't even play football, and like the

fashion side of things: 'Oh yeah, did you see what Leah Williamson was wearing?' Things like that. This is crazy.

"I'm not bitter about it. That's the thing. I want to embrace it. I think it's fantastic. Some people are a bit like, 'Oh, well, it wasn't like that [before]'. It had to start somewhere, isn't it? It literally did.

"And I guess I feel like I was lucky enough to taste the professional set-up by going to Florida. I got to taste what it was like to be training every day, being flown around the country, being given and living that life, and so I'll always hold that dear."

⚽

"I'll tell everyone, like, 'My pal Dan Murph, she's a fire-fighter.' I'll tell everyone that. I am proper proud, like that job takes a lot of balls to do."

Not only was Cope proud of Murphy, but she remained very fond of her and her two children ("When I saw her, and I saw that bump, I had to actually just check it wasn't a football there because I was thinking, 'This ain't Dan!' – I was gobsmacked!").

"I remember saying to her when she was studying – she used to have all her study cards on the coach, going to away games – 'Dan, if there's a fire, proper fire, like, don't you go in. Don't go in, Dan, please!'" she laughed.

"She's a good kid, Dan. She's still my baby sister."

Cope had been doing the same numbers on the National Lottery since its inception, and was laughingly sure they would win the jackpot for her soon ("It better bloody hurry up!"). When the cheque came in, she said, there were some surprise lump sums earmarked for three of her closest friends in football, one of whom was Murphy.

"I'll go round their house, not telling them [I've won the lottery], just chatting. Then I'll go, 'Dan, how much you got left on your mortgage?' and I'll just write a cheque – 'Go on, mate, pay off your mortgage.'"

"She could nutmeg a mermaid."

It was an unusual metaphor, but the opinion was plain to see. Wales's long-time record goal-scorer, a striker who had graced the shirts of both Arsenal and Chelsea in her time, Helen Ward (nee Lander) had never seen a better technical player than Ellen Maggs.

It would not be overstating it to say that Maggs was not well known, yet she had played in England teams alongside Casey Stoney, Laura Bassett, Sue Smith and Faye White, and for Arsenal with Lianne Sanderson, Alex Scott and Anita Asante. Islington born and bred, she had first come to the attention of Gunners scouts when they were running sessions in local schools. She joined the club as an under-9, and held a season ticket for the men's team, going to then-home ground Highbury regularly to support her team. At the age of sixteen, she left school and began working at the club as a trainee, learning how to coach. All this, plus pulling on the red and white every Sunday to represent the club – Maggs was living every supporter's dream, and had surely fulfilled all her childhood ambitions by the time she turned seventeen.

Maggs's relative lack of celebrity can be explained by the fact that she spent much of her footballing career in the shadow of one of the all-time greats, Kelly Smith. The two played in the same position, and, Maggs reflected, she always thought Smith would be selected ahead of her, no matter who the coach was or what the match might be. When Maggs knew that Smith was returning to England and likely to Arsenal following a stellar college career in the USA, she considered her options, ultimately signing for Birmingham City and their manager Marcus Bignot.

"I watched Kelly play, which was a joy, but I had the feeling that she was going to come back [to Arsenal], and that would be me not needed at Arsenal," she explained. Some friends put her in touch with Bignot, who talked about his plans for Birmingham City, and she was amazed to learn that there would be money on offer for players. "At the time, I was still working at the club, at Arsenal. I was working in the laundry by this point, I was at the men's training ground, cleaning all the kit, so the idea of going to Birmingham, and they'd pay me the same amount of money as what I was getting to play and to work in the laundry, just to play, and the fact that Kelly was coming, I just went, 'That's a good idea.'"

However, the big plans did not quite transpire as they had expected. The financial support was not quite there, and Bignot's own footballing career began to get in the way of his coaching responsibilities. The experienced players he had signed did not quite gel with the youngsters coming through the youth ranks (many of whom became big names themselves within the decade, such as Karen Carney and Eniola Aluko). At the end of the first season of Bignot's project, Rachel Yankey and Alex Scott signed for Arsenal, with another England international, Amanda Barr, opting to return to Doncaster Belles. Maggs stayed on for one more season, and then decided to retire, at the age of twenty-three. The combination of needing to work another job and the travel from London was simply too much for her, and she ended up coaching for Yankey's soccer school in the neighbouring borough of Brent, and then working in a nursery, caring for children and cleaning the building.

It was Sian Williams who revitalised Maggs's career.

"She's an absolute hero," said Maggs. "She was my idol growing up as well. When I was playing in and around Arsenal, Sian was the one. She was such a good footballer: small, technically good, I was like, 'That's what I want to be.'

"She became the manager of Watford and just said, 'It's silly you're not playing. You should be coming to play for us.'

"They weren't in the top division, they were the division below. 'We only train one day a week. We play matches on the Sundays, and that's it. That's your only commitment. If you can't make training, can't make it, don't worry, you'll be all right.'"

It was also Williams who put Maggs in touch with the owners of New York Magic, who were seeking players for their squad in the summer of 2006. Playing in the USA was not something she had ever considered; describing her as a homebody would be an understatement.

"When I tell you I never left Islington before that, you won't believe me. I haven't left it since either. I didn't know I had it in me," she said.

New York and London might both be busy cities, but apart from anything else the climate was very different and meant the training schedule was quite unusual.

"It was so hot. You had to wait for the sun to go down, so all training was evenings, all matches were evenings, but it was a fantastic experience," said Maggs. "We had a nice little apartment in New York, but never even had a kitchen in it, because no one cooks in New York apparently. Everyone goes out. Everyone goes out for dinner. So there wasn't even a place to cook a meal or anything. It was just like, 'There's a bed for you, there's a bed for you, there's a bed for you.'"

Indeed, the club management took their overseas players out for dinner every night, and their new team-mates would invite them round to socialise, often with a pool party as so many of them had swimming pools at their homes as standard – something else that Maggs found hard to believe.

Strangely, she did not even play all her games for Magic up front. The first-choice goalkeeper was missing for a handful of matches, and the coach asked for a volunteer to go between the sticks. Maggs – at a height of five feet and two inches, or 157 cm – was the first to put her hand up. It was no wonder that everyone else looked at her rather askance before agreeing.

"I loved it! I trained goalkeeper every week. Emma Byrne was the goalkeeper at Arsenal, and Vic had sorted out the goalkeeping training with the academy boys for Emma. So she was training with the [under-]16 and [under-]18 goalies, with [coach] Alex Welsh. I used to go along and I used to join in and I used to love it, do all the handling, everything.

"In a different life, if I was taller, I would have been a goal-keeper, that's my favourite position."

"She was really crazy about Arsenal. I think she was, yes, yes, yes, yes, a great player. But she's also an easy-to-get-along-[with] personality.

"She was one of them that adapted. She was very adapt-able: that would be a good word to describe it, adaptable in soccer, adaptable in life. She just kind of went with the flow."

Despite the years that had passed, Ellen Maggs was still fresh in the memory of Lyndelle Phillips, who founded New York Magic alongside partner and head coach Nino DePasquali. He remembered Maggs well too.

"She was a very good defender, very coachable," he said.

Phillips interjected: "I didn't think Maggs was a defender!"

DePasquali, unabashed, replied: "A defender. I played her in defence."

DePasquali's decades in the women's game had given him a fascinating global perspective; he looked at what players could offer and slotted them into a system, rather than being boxed in by the position they thought they were stuck in. ("'I'm a forward! I'm a striker!' Yeah, you are a striker – [but] play where I ask you to play.") For someone like Maggs, willing to play wherever he asked, and to try out different positions, his philosophy was perfect; it was no wonder that he described her as "very coachable". There were some characteristics he thought were shared by players brought up in particular countries. In the USA, fitness was key: "Everything is based on physicality… for sure, they can run. They can run from six o'clock in the morning to midnight, then if they can play soccer, it's another story." His favourite type of players were ones who were "very good from the neck up"; indeed, he pinpointed Sian Williams as one of the two most intelligent players he ever coached.

Between DePasquali and Phillips, they had created one of the longest-running women's football teams in the country. In a world where women's leagues sprouted and then melted away, and clubs changed their names and home catchment areas, this was remarkable longevity. DePasquali was a former professional player; Phillips began playing the game when she was at school, and became involved with the sport's administration when she moved to New York. She merged her knowledge of law, regulations and process with DePasquali's professional background in the sport, and launched New York Magic.

When they started out, Phillips recalled, the United Soccer Leagues were looking to create a national football footprint – much like the FA did when they set up the Women's National League rather than regionalised competitions.

"I just know that when the players were coming over, they didn't have the same options in England that we had here in terms of the levels of competition."

The United Women's Soccer League, to which New York Magic belonged for sixteen years, had many other clubs that also attracted players from overseas. Many British coaches had gone to the USA to work in college football, knowing they could carve out a career in the women's game, and then encouraged players they knew from back home to try a spell in the USA. Phillips also thought that word of mouth carried fast between players in the UK – although she called it "word of organisation", explaining: "New York Magic was an opportunity and an outlet."

Some players opted to stay in the USA, applying for college and making a life out there. As Phillips put it, "Maggs didn't. Maggs came, played, went home."

She did not, however, think that homesickness ever impacted on Maggs's life in New York.

"I think she realised that this might be a once-in-a-lifetime opportunity. She took the best of it. Most of what [the British players] wanted to do was go through New York City, check out everything that's going on in New York, play soccer, travel with the team. It was a whirlwind, doing what you enjoy doing."

Players were still staying in the same apartments that Maggs and others of her generation had lived in. As Phillips wryly noted: "If Maggs and those guys [did] come back, [they'd be] like, 'Oh, you've still got this table!'"

Yet playing for clubs such as Magic had become less attractive for British players, Phillips thought; with the women's professional game taking hold in England and to a much lesser degree in Scotland, there were more opportunities without having to travel. It was ironic, Phillips pointed out, that now there were more American players who wanted to head to Europe rather than the opposite direction of travel.

"They want to play in Spain, they want to play in Germany, they want to play in France. But at the time, people were coming here, and it was to experience soccer, because the United States, at that point, they were winning cups. They were the country that I think gave more financial backing and funding for the development of women's soccer. And so people were really looking to expand and explore opportunities and options here, and when they came, they were able to play the sport that they love."

Maggs spent just the single summer out there, and then returned to the UK to play for Watford, never even considering the possibility of extending her stay.

"It's funny, I played in the [first] under-19 World Cup [now the under-20 World Cup], which was in Canada [in 2002], and had a couple of offers, from Harvard University and another one, about going over there on a scholarship, like a college programme, but I was the worst studier you have ever come across. I could not wait to leave school and get out of it. I was just like, 'Thanks, but no thanks.' Didn't even think anything of it.

"When I came back [from Canada, people said,] 'Oh, my God, you have to do it!' No, I really don't! It meant nothing to me, being there or going to do it. So, yeah, I had no intentions of doing it for longer or going back again. It was like, 'I've done it now, I can go home.'"

This mindset, she thought, was also why she did not get more caps for England. Aside from the competition with Kelly Smith for one spot in the starting line-up, she did not enjoy the necessary travel or being away from home; she simply enjoyed playing football, and if she could not do that then she did not see the point of being part of a squad.

"My first call-up was against France. [France striker] Thierry Henry was my sponsor at Arsenal at the time, and I remember doing a big photo shoot with him about it being England-France and him sponsoring me and that being my first England call-up – and I went away [with the England camp] and then just stood in the stand watching everyone play football. I didn't even get in the squad. What's this? I could have been at home!

"I didn't really fit in: going away for a week. I enjoyed the training, enjoyed being around everybody, [but] not playing, it's difficult for me. I always wanted to play every minute of every game. I wanted to play. So it's like, 'There's no point me coming here and not playing. I'd rather stay and play at Arsenal, they'll have a game, or someone will have a game somewhere.' So I struggled to get the right mentality to be an

England international. I finally started getting some minutes. I was coming on, I was at least making the bench, or I was coming on as sub, and then I finally got a start and came off at half-time, and then I was, 'I just don't think this is for me.'"

Her senior England career drew naturally to a close, and lasted less than eighteen months. She finished with four caps; after her first substitute appearance in May 2003 – replacing her old Birmingham pal Amanda Barr – she made one start, in February 2003 against Denmark, when she was named in the eleven alongside long-standing rival Kelly Smith. An unused substitute on three occasions, Maggs made her final appearance as a substitute in September 2004. She admitted that England coach Hope Powell had spoken to her more than once in an effort to get her to work harder or train more.

"Hope always wanted me to do more, she wanted me to go to the gym more, she wanted me to enjoy being there more, and I just couldn't do it. She was like, 'You are the most frustrating player I have ever coached. I do not believe you haven't got any motivation.'

"'You know what? I don't, and I can't dig deep enough to find that. I don't want it enough, and that sounds terrible, but I'm quite happy not playing for England.'"

England were hosting the 2005 European Championships, and in the camp prior to the squad being named, Maggs was given another nudge.

"Hope was like, 'You're going to have to really work hard if you want to get in the squad.' I was like, 'I'm not sure I want to,' and then I never got in.

"The letter [announcing the squad] came through, and I remember opening it, and my mum was with me when I opened it, and it was like, 'You're on standby,' and I was like, 'Oh, thank God for that,' and Mum was like, 'What do you mean? What's wrong with you?!' I knew then I'm done here. That was when I was like, I've had enough."

The end of her England career came in the middle of her two seasons with Williams at Watford, after which Maggs stepped away from football again, this time for the best part of a decade. Playing and working was draining her, and the rigours and routine of going to training with matches every weekend meant she started to lose her love for the game. She was encouraged back into it after the birth of her nephew, with her sister telling her that she would have to take him to matches; and then, while working as a nanny, one of the boys she cared for began training with a local football school. Maggs went along to watch one of the sessions, and found herself offering to run a girls-only session for them. Her mission now was to expand grassroots football for girls, leading training sessions, supporting clubs and helping to set up leagues to encourage a competitive pathway for those that wanted it: all in London, while still living in the same house in which she grew up. It felt almost like Maggs had come home – not geographically, but London girls' grassroots football was where her heart lay. She may have been one of the most technically gifted players of her generation that few had even heard of, but she was satisfied with her footballing achievements.

As for regrets, she found it tough to pinpoint many, although she did wonder how her career may have turned out if she had made one different decision.

"When I was doing my job at Arsenal, and I was a trainee, I was the only girl on the course. I was playing football with boys every day, and in that period of playing football with boys every day, in that two-year period, I broke into the Arsenal first team, I broke into the England first team, and that's probably the best I've been. I think leaving that job or that role, and not trying to stay in that for a further year, was probably where I went wrong, because I think training and playing with the boys every day, I enjoyed it, and it made me a better player, and that got me there, and I think had I continued to do that, I probably could have gone further or done more.

"But, you know, I travelled loads, met loads of fantastic people. If I had the chance to go back now, knowing that [the women's game] goes professional, I probably still wouldn't have had the motivation and the love and the enjoyment to do it. So I'm not sure that much would have changed. So I like to look back and think I achieved what I could have, I got far in the game, and then I got a real job and a real life."

With her comparatively low profile, it would be easy to overlook quite how much Maggs did achieve in the game, from league titles to cup wins as well as her international recognition and her time abroad.

"I did everything I could have wanted to. I played at the top level, played in the Champions League for Arsenal the very first season it existed. I played for England, played in the World Cup in the under-19s. I don't go on holidays, so the only travelling I've ever done is through football, I don't have a passport any more. So without all of that, I'd prob- ably would have got to this point and thought, 'What have I done in my life?' Having all of that, I look back and go, 'I've done enough. I'm happy.'"

MANAGER

Coaching was Pauline Hamill's passion from an early age. She took jobs in factories and elsewhere to make ends meet alongside her playing career, but she particularly loved coaching, from grassroots level upwards.

"I really enjoyed helping other people, even as a player, trying to understand what my role was in the team, and I was always wanting to help people on the pitch with their role. I was fascinated with what they had to do as well."

She had coached the junior teams in the Scotland set-up while still a senior player herself, was head of girls' and women's football at Falkirk for five years, and performance academy manager at the University of Stirling at the end of her playing career.

It was a garlanded playing career, too. She had played football with boys her entire life. From the moment she could run, she thought, she had a ball at her feet, out in the street with her playmates from the houses nearby. She was good at a lot of sports, but football was the one she loved. She had no idea that, at the same time that she was forming a team with her male friends, the likes of Edna Neillis and Rose Reilly were struggling to play football in Scotland at all.

"I had no idea of anything outwith playing with the boys

and loving it," she said. At the age of fifteen, her father saw an advert for a girls' team that were about twenty minutes' drive away. "I was coming to that age where things were getting to be a little bit different, because [the boys] were all men, built like men, and physically, for me, it was getting really tough."

Hamill joined Coltness as an attacking midfielder or striker, and her eyes were opened to the tough situation female footballers in Scotland had faced – and continued to face. Conversely, though, she also began to realise the opportunities she could have.

"There were women leading that team who had been national team players in the past – they were in the latter stages of their career in that moment – and they were the ones who were driving this new club forward.

"They were chatting to me about the potential that I had. I just loved to play – I wasn't really concerned about my potential."

One of Scotland's leading teams Cumbernauld asked Hamill to join them one year later, and her mindset had completely changed.

"I really wanted to be the best by that point; I wanted to train and play with the best.

"See, when I was just playing with boys, I never really realised how good I was. That was just what I did: I played football every day, and there were no other girls around me, so I had no idea.

"I actually remember as a really young kid, being on holiday with Mum and Dad, and I remember walking along the beach.

"My dad said to me, 'What do you think you want to do in your life, Pauline?' and I was only maybe about eleven or twelve, and I said, 'Do you know, Dad, I'm not really bothered what I do, but I would love to play for Scotland.'

"Don't ask me why I thought that at that moment, because I really don't know. Football was always on in our house. My dad was football crazy, and he said to me, 'Well, do you know what? We'll do all we can to try to help you.'

"He must have known that I had some level of potential. My dad was always really quiet and unassuming, and stood back and just let me enjoy. If I was playing a match and scored five goals, they would say, 'Well done. Did you enjoy it?' If I didn't have my best game, 'Did you enjoy it? Was it good fun? Well done.' It was never anything about 'You're this good', so as a young person, I was just playing football.

"Then when I went to Coltness, I started to realise I was really good because I was different from all the other players. I was never comfortable with that, because in many ways, I just wanted to be the same as the rest of the players. But I wasn't, and it was quite obvious that I wasn't, whenever I went to training. I could do more things than anybody else could do in matches against whoever we played; even when we played in the cup against the top teams, I was always the best player, always scoring goals, and so it was obvious that I was quite different to everyone else.

"In that year [at Coltness] for me, I thought, 'Well, if I'm this good, and everybody's telling me I'm this good, I'm going to try and go for it, and try to see how good I can be, and how good I can become.'"

From there, it was a trajectory to the top of the game. During a stellar career in her homeland, she represented Stenhousemuir, Kilmarnock, Hibernian, Spartans and Celtic, and got the international recognition that she wanted and that her coaches at Coltness had predicted years previously. She was the first woman to win 100 caps for Scotland, making 141 appearances over eighteen years with the national team, the most by any player, male or female, by the time she retired. She also spent time in England with Doncaster Belles and with Blackburn Rovers, and a season in Iceland with IBV.

She was already an experienced player and on the verge of turning thirty by the time she accepted the unusual and unexpected offer to head to Iceland in 2001. Her friend and team-mate Michelle Barr had already agreed to join IBV, and asked if she fancied coming to watch a match in England.

"She said, 'Do you want to come down to down south with me for the journey? I'm going to go and play in this match before heading out to Iceland. The coaches said, 'Bring your boots if you want to bring your boots.'

"And I said, 'Right, I'll come with you.' I was thinking, 'OK, it's a good day out. We'll go. I'll watch my pal playing football, and maybe I'll take my boots.'

"So I took my boots in the car and I went down, and something happened, they had a couple of injuries, and the coach said to me, 'Do you want to play some time?'

"Now, I wasn't ready to play, but I said, 'Yeah, OK, that's fine,' and I went and played, and as soon as I played, I came off the pitch, and they said to me, 'Do you want to come over to Iceland for the summer?'

"I gave it some thought going home, then we had further discussions, and then I thought, 'Why not?' They played a summer league. I was only going to be away for six months. So it's a new experience, a new league, new people, a new environment. Everything about it is something to experience in your lifetime, so I agreed to go."

She remembered Sammy Britton very well.

"Wee Sammy stayed in the apartment below me. What a girl she is! Absolutely hilarious. I loved her experience, the person she was, the character, everything she brought to the team.

"And she loved [the singer] Tracy Chapman. In the mornings she used to play Tracy Chapman, and I always said to her, 'You're my alarm clock. As soon as Tracy Chapman comes on, that's my chance to get up.'"

Hamill remembered the Icelandic league as a strong one, with many of their international players taking part.

"The level at that moment was higher than the level in Scotland. It was a lot of players that were committing their own time: we were full-time players in that team, but a lot of the Icelandic girls were working, and then they were coming to training at five o'clock; whereas when I was there, I wasn't working, I was just having all the time to invest in my training, and playing, and recovery."

It was a chance she had never had previously.

"You're working full time and you're trying to train full time [in Scotland], and it was so difficult. So for me [in Iceland], I go from that to I'm up at the club in the morning, I can take the balls out, I used to go and practice my finishing, I used to practice driving with a ball in the mornings, train in the afternoons. I could go to the jacuzzi at lunchtime and sit and relax my muscles, and eat well. I'm in this environment that I've never experienced before. It was hardly any surprise that the performance levels were high, because all you were doing was focusing on football. It was something that could have lasted a lot longer, but for me at the time that one year was fitting into my life plan."

She also remembered the island of Vestmannaeyjar just as fondly as Britton had: "It's such a small place, that island. The people were amazing. They couldn't have made us feel more welcome. If you ever get a chance, go to that island, because it's something you would have to experience in your lifetime. You're in the middle of the ocean and walk up this big hill, and on the other side is just the ocean. They've got everything in this community that you could ever need or want for kids to do sport or go to school and the shops, and it's just a fantastic place to see."

Michelle Barr won every honour possible in the Scottish game in a career that saw her represent Cumbernauld, Stenhousemuir, Kilmarnock, Celtic and Rangers. A strong central defender, she also picked up 87 international caps:

a testament to her constant search for ways to improve her game.

With the domestic league in Scotland still amateur, lagging behind near neighbours England, her first spell overseas was in 1999 with Miami Gliders, giving her a taste of semi-professional football in the USL W-League. She travelled to the USA with three other Scottish players, with whom she shared an apartment just off South Beach.

Barr's next foray out of Scotland to play her club football was two years later, and meant a relatively short journey – crossing the border into England to join Doncaster Belles. It was a team-mate of hers there – Karen Burke – who laid the foundation for her move further afield, although it would not have happened had it not been for another player's last-minute rethink.

"We were good friends, Karen and I, and we played in the same team in England; we played for Doncaster Belles together, and then we also played at Leeds together, so we'd been friends for a long time. She had [been to Iceland to play for IBV], so she put me in touch with the coach. There were four of us actually looking to go, and they only needed three players, and I was late to the party, as they say!

"But then one of the players pulled out and was like, 'I don't know if I can go and live away from home and do all that,' and then he called me up and was like, 'We're actually looking for a centre back. Would you want to come?'

"It just happened like that. Karen was in her second year, Sammy Britton [was there]... and so I decided to go. What have I got to lose? I mean, like I said, if I don't like it, I will just go home. It's an hour and a half to go home on a flight."

Barr felt no inkling of homesickness at all. Of course she enjoyed being able to train every day and play in a competitive league, improving her game little by little, but she also loved living in Iceland, settling happily in Vestmannaeyjar for the next three years. Because Iceland's league ran over the summer, she would play the season, and then return to the UK for a few months to play in the winter competition there, spending a season with Belles, moving to Kilmarnock in 2002, back to Belles in 2003, and Leeds United in 2004.

"I went [to Iceland for the second year in March] when it was really dark – regretted that initially! I was like, 'Wait, you don't have any sunlight here!' But I went in March to get to do a pre-season with them.

"I was on a small island, Vestmannaeyjar, twenty minutes from Reykjavik by flight – it was either flight or boat, and the boat was three hours from the mainland. I lived on the island for four years. I went back and forward. I was playing with the national team at the time, and then the winter months, I came back to Britain and played.

"It was a great level [in Iceland] at the time. I felt it was a step up for me, because I was [originally] playing in Scotland, but I was playing with the national team, and the team I was playing for in Scotland, we were winning every single year, and I was a centre back, and I just felt that I wasn't being challenged enough. I wanted to get better, and that's no disrespect to anyone that was there: I just wanted to get better – within my team, I could, but against the level of opponent."

Barr was greeted at Reykjavik airport by one of the IBV club committee, who then took her on to the island and showed her to her apartment that she shared with the two others who had come from Scotland. They were also provided with a car, and were paid a monthly salary along with bonuses for various accomplishments including progress in cup competitions: "They provided everything for us, so we never really had to worry."

One of her team-mates there was Sammy Britton, whose original thinking stuck in Barr's memory.

"We had a few laughs playing with Sammy Britton, that's for sure, never a dull moment. I went into her apartment one day and she had black bin liners up in the windows.

"'Sammy, what's going on?'

"'Well, Michelle, it's twenty-four-hours-a-day light here. I can't sleep at night, so I'm blocking the sunlight out.'

"OK, that makes sense. Good player, but we had some laughs, for sure!"

IBV had plenty of other good players at the time as well, winning the country's premier cup competition for the first time in their history. The squad won the final in Reykjavik, beating Valur 2–0, and then had to fly back to Vestmannaeyjar amidst bad weather – a journey Barr remembered vividly.

"There were people throwing up and everything, the weather was awful," she said, adding a thank you to the skill of the crew, obviously used to flying in storms and snow. "However, they do say Icelandic pilots are the best – it's probably for that reason!"

Her next move was one that developed her coaching skills as well as her on-pitch abilities, spending another summer in the USA, this time with Vermont Lady Voltage, while coaching at Dartmouth College, a prestigious tertiary school. Angie Hind, who had been a Scotland team-mate, invited Barr out to assist on some summer camps, and, when she got the role of head coach at the college, then asked Barr to consider applying for it. She got the job, and spent five years there, hanging up her playing boots except for a brief spell with Boston Renegades, before returning to Scotland to coach with the junior national teams and to scout for the seniors.

"I've always been very passionate about making a difference in my own country, about helping the game grow and to develop players, so I was super interested in doing that," she explained. She decided to start playing again, first for Celtic, then for Rangers, before opting to retire at the age of thirty-five. The thought kept crossing her mind that, although she loved working with the national team players, especially the young talent, she really only got to coach them infrequently, when they were on camp, and what she really wanted to do was coach every day and help them develop. Serendipity intervened once more, with Hind appointed as head coach at Old Dominion Monarchs in 2014, and inviting her old team-mate to join her once again. By the summer of 2024, Barr was associate head coach, leading on player development, and really immersed in her major interest.

MANAGER

Thoroughly settled in the USA, she was well aware – from her time coaching in Scotland – that British coaches could still be very wary if a player expressed a wish to experience another footballing culture for any reason, even to pursue an academic course in conjunction with playing.

"Sometimes people back home don't understand the level of football in [different] areas. So at that time [around 2010], America was deemed as, 'Oh, you can't go there. They're not good at soccer, they're very athletic, they don't pass the ball, they don't possess the ball.'

"In my time, there wasn't a whole lot of people going away. I was one of the first. It depends on the player and the situation. I just felt I needed to move to get better, and I'd already been in England, so it was a little bit different for me, I'm really doing the same thing, but just moving to another different country. As long it's a good level and you can get back and forward for [international matches] then I think, 'Why wouldn't you?'

"The best scenario is to have everyone play in Scotland. Of course it is. But the problem is we just don't have the resources. We don't have the facilities. We don't have the weather all the time to be able to have a league that's super competitive. Even the league now in Scotland, we have two, three, four teams, I would say now, that have professional players in training every day. It's taken a long time for that to happen: too long, in my opinion. If you look at the players that get selected for the national team, half of them are out the country, so that doesn't help [with improving the quality and professionalism of the Scottish league]. Our best players are leaving to go and play at a better level, because they just don't have the product in Scotland to keep them there."

Of course, many were following the path carved by the likes of Barr, heading just over the border to England to play in the WSL. She pointed to her former Rangers team-mate Erin Cuthbert, who joined Chelsea as a teenager, as a prime example.

"She loves it there. It's a tough one. You don't want your best players leaving the country. It would be ideal for them all to be training every day and playing in Scotland every day, and we would have a league where we have twelve teams that are really competitive. Right now we don't have that.

"It's kind of sad in a way. I feel that that side of things should be far advanced, far more advanced than it is. All that's going to happen now is the teams [at the top] are going to pull away."

Barr's desire for her native country to advance applied to coaching as well; there simply were not enough jobs in women's football there for an ambitious person who wanted to work with players on a daily basis. The USA's huge collegiate programme offered plenty of opportunities, and the climate in Norfolk, Virginia, meant lots of time out on the training pitches.

"We're lucky here. We have the weather. We can be on the field every day. We don't have to be indoors or anything. Very rarely do we get any crazy weather or snow or anything, the part of Virginia that I'm in, but you just get to see [the players] develop, both as people, which is really, really nice and really important if you have them three or four years, and then also as players. We're on the field every day with them, and that's what I'm passionate about. I like to coach. I like to help make them better. I like to see them grow. I love all the other stuff, all the scouting and the recruiting, video analysis, all that stuff, but the thing that excites me the most, and that I enjoy, is being around them and coaching and helping them develop, and unfortunately, I can't do that in Scotland."

The resources Barr and other collegiate coaches were able to draw upon were immense. With large amounts of travel required for teams to get to away games and tournaments, rather than using buses or minibuses – as would be the case in the UK – they would fly. Players were supported to keep up with their courses, with academic advisors on hand if needed, but Barr was quick to point out that soccer practice took up only a couple of hours a day, in the mornings, with the rest of the day available for study. She felt that the USA remained an excellent option for a young British player hoping to make a career in the professional game; with the success of the Women's Super League in England, superstars from around the world were attracted to it, meaning fewer and fewer chances for homegrown players to progress quickly to the first team.

"This is an avenue: 'OK, I'm not ready for the full team right now. I've come out the under-18s or the [under-]21s, whatever, not quite ready to make that step.' Then they could come here, for two years, four years, and study, get their degree, and obviously play and develop at the same time, because in the right environment, you will absolutely develop here.

"It's not just soccer or" – Barr corrected her use of the American term – "sorry, football. It's not just that. It's everything else that comes with it: the athletic training that they have, the sports science that they have. We have everything, they're in the gym as well, we have strength coaches. They get everything they need to succeed at this level."

The American league, the NWSL, was well established and, combined with the consistency of the US women's national team at World Cups and Olympic Games, it maintained the USA's position as a desirable destination for the female aspiring footballer, regardless of her nationality. Barr was careful to point out that even the USA had its challenges when it came to women's football, and did not guarantee a route from college to the professional league. Canada was another possibility for a football player already in North America, and ironically Barr and her colleague Angie Hind were also more than happy to link players up with clubs in Europe should they be interested in a move there. Migration in the women's professional game – one way or another – was by now common if not entirely expected.

"We've had a lot of players go and play professionally after [college]. So it's a really good appeal to come here, because if you're someone that does want to play pro, then we can certainly help [you], and we do nothing but encourage that. It breaks my heart when the players come in and play for four years, and they're really good, and then one day, once they graduate, they're like, 'OK, Coach, I'm done.'

"I'm like, 'Why would you not keep playing?'

"'Well, I'm going to go be a math teacher.'

"'The world's always going to need math teachers. Why don't you still play for the next five years and then be a math teacher?' There's so many avenues now where you can get paid [for playing football]."

⚽

Hamill's coaching career had more recently moved from Scotland to Saudi Arabia, a move she said had come "completely out of the blue". With money being invested in the women's game's infrastructure there, the governing body were specifically looking for female coaches with the highest possible qualification, the UEFA Pro Licence, to assist with setting up their clubs. Hamill had initially turned the role down, but was then approached about coaching the women's under-20s squad.

"It started to really interest me, for lots of different reasons," she said, "and as I started to meet the leadership group and the technical team, I just thought, 'You know what? What is the worst thing that can happen here? I can come home.'"

She agreed to take the job in 2023, and was shuttling from team camps back to her home in Scotland, not wishing to disrupt her family. She had had other offers to manage senior teams, but youth development was her passion.

"I think that's something I can do really well. Having been an ex-player, it definitely gives you some kind of starting point. Many people think you can only be a good coach if you've been a player. I don't particularly agree with that, but for me, it gave me an understanding of what it's like to be a young female and coming up through youth football, and I had a real interest in psychology and how girls and women are affected as they come through a pathway that's on a performance level. I really had a love for coaching from a very early stage, but I was coaching on a performance level with the under-15 national team when I was still a player, and I just could see the difference I could make to players, and I had a real understanding of their journey, and I knew what they were going through. All of that, alongside building up your expertise and knowledge as a coach and learning from all the people around you: all of those things form who you are."

She had certainly seen a big change in the Scotland set-up for female players over the course of her career on and off the pitch. She recalled being given training and match kit that looked and felt cheap, and did not fit correctly ("You put your money into your pocket, and the pocket went away down to your ankle, and if there had been a box of matches near you, you would have been up in flames!"). She gave a great deal of credit to former national team coach Vera Pauw – Jeannie Allott's team-mate at KFC '71 – who was in post from 1998 to 2004.

"Here was this woman coming in that knew everything

about every player in the world, and our preparations suddenly went up a notch, and she knew everything about opponent analysis. I was mesmerised by this person. She was on a level of knowledge that I'd certainly never experienced in my life. She really took us from a group of people to a team, and let us understand more tactically how it all worked on the pitch.

"She started to push and push, and her character was such that she would never take no for an answer, and sometimes working in a male-dominated environment, that comes across in a different way: knowing men start to get fed up with you because you keep chapping the door, and they think that then you're a problem, but actually they're the problem, because the fact you have to chap the door tells you everything."

Players always owed a debt of gratitude to their predecessors, Hamill thought, and that was particularly true for Scottish women, whose path had been carved by Rose Reilly, Edna Neillis and their contemporaries.

"We always have to be really thankful to Rose Reilly and the people in her generation, because they did things to promote the sport that we could probably never imagined, what they had to do to really drag the sport out of the way it was… the way it had to be dragged kicking and screaming to give women a platform to play for the national team.

"For those people to do what they did, for me, I'm just in awe of what they did. They gave me a chance to then impact in the way that I could. It just continues like that.

You just want there to be the next generation of people who are really going to fight, because there'll still be fights to be had.

"I'm sure it's improved, but not without women at the forefront who are really pushing and fighting and making sure that these things happen for the next generation."

EPILOGUE

For decades, women's football in Britain lagged behind many other countries. That was not due to a lack of talent, but a lack of recognition; it was treated as a sideshow, a novelty, a distraction from the serious business of the men's game. That was not to say that matters were ideal for women's football in other countries, simply that they were a better option than staying at home. With so few options for the gifted female footballer in Britain, it is fascinating to see how many opportunities opened up to them once they cast their eyes further afield to a more forward-thinking, innovative league. That was not to say that they necessarily always had the chance to play football and earn a decent living from it, but they certainly had more options to combine football with a more flexible day job that understood the sacrifices that top-class sport required, or to even be a full-time player, concentrating only on matches and training, with everything else provided by the club. Intriguingly, many of these countries would have described their own native players as amateurs

– think of Kerry Davis waiting for her Lazio team-mates to finish work so that they could train, for example. Often it was only the overseas players who were looked after to such a degree.

In 1989, Jane Stanley, two months into her spell playing for Standard Liege in Belgium, was described as "England's only professional woman footballer" by the *Scarborough Evening News* in her home town. She had been a sports assistant with the local council, playing up front for Filey Flyers, before being spotted by talent scouts while playing in an international tournament in France, who offered her a three-year contract. Asked for her thoughts on whether such opportunities might arise in England in the near future, she replied: "I don't think it'll happen for another hundred years."

The quotes between sections of this book are taken from the post-match interviews after England lost in the quarter-final of their first-ever Women's World Cup in 1995, defeated 3–0 by the mighty Germany. These short excerpts show how starkly aware the England squad were that other countries were far ahead of them in terms of fitness, coaching and strength in depth of players they were able to call on. It was no wonder that so many of them spent time overseas; despite Ted Copeland's optimistic suggestions that the players needed to adjust their aspirations and perform like the leading footballing nations, the players – like captain Debbie Bampton, who played in Italy – hinted broadly that they knew very well that the domestic game in England needed a serious overhaul in the future should its representative national team ever wish to compete on equal terms at an elite level.

Just a few years after Ellen Maggs and Dan Murphy came back from the USA, collegiate football became the smart move for any female footballer from the UK who had dreams of playing at the top. The so-called "draft" system there meant that on the conclusion of their studies, top collegiate players could be assigned to the rosters of a professional team, giving them a clear career path. Although the Women's United Soccer Association, a professional league, ran for only three seasons, between 2001 and 2003, by 2009 Women's Professional Soccer, or WPS, was up and running. That too closed within three years, but the National Women's Soccer League (NWSL) launched in 2012 and continues to thrive.

By this time, this talent drain from Britain to foreign leagues had finally been noticed and, crucially, highlighted as something that needed to be stopped. The FA, who had been closely watching the operation of the American professional leagues, wanted their best female players to stay in England and improve the quality and competitiveness of the domestic league rather than flying across the Atlantic or taking a short jaunt on to the continent and adorning one of the European leagues. They launched the Women's Super League in 2011 – a football competition quite unlike any that the British football fan would be used to. To avoid any single team dominating, as had happened in the years before, England players were shared around the clubs, and there was no relegation into a lower division. Instead, the eight teams were geographically spread around the country, enticing more fans through the turnstiles, and with no threat of relegation, clubs were guaranteed their spotlight and thus stability. The players were on paid contracts, although many bolstered their comparatively limited playing income with additional jobs.

The 2012 London Olympic Games marked a real leap into the mainstream for British women's football, brought together for the first time to compete for Team GB. Three years later, England's third-place finish at the Women's World Cup in Canada attracted millions of viewers, even with the unhelpful time difference in the UK, meaning fans had to stay up late to watch some of the matches.

Of course, the appointment of Sarina Wiegman – Jeannie Allott's former team-mate – as England head coach marked the start of a rocket-fuelled rise to the very top of the game. She led her Lionesses to European glory in 2022, following that up with a Women's World Cup final in 2023, with her players becoming chat-show guests, quiz-show panellists, magazine cover stars, podcast hosts and more as their celebrity grew. The WSL had finally turned fully professional in 2018, with the Professional Footballers' Association, the country's players' union, setting up a women's game department in 2020; and a new independent company took over responsibility for both the top tier and the second tier Women's Championship in the summer of 2024, demonstrating just how much the women's game had grown and its new requirement for commercial and business expertise separate from the men's competitions. Any gifted English girl now would have the ambition to play for a WSL club and represent the Lionesses, and this would be a plausible career path.

Yet the trailblazers in this book also hail from the rest of the UK. It is easy to conflate 'English' with 'British' when it comes to football. The English leagues have always lured in the best talent from other parts of the British Isles, in men's and women's football, to the detriment of the other domestic competitions, who have been left playing catch-up. So it has proved with the wide-ranging impact of the WSL. Of the twenty-three in the Scotland squad who played in their first-ever Women's World Cup in 2019, sixteen of them played their club football outside the country, twelve of them in England. That was despite the establishment of a women's national academy, based at the University of Stirling, meaning young players had the chance to train and play every day, and benefit from top-class coaching, under the eye of Pauline Hamill, who had herself played overseas in Iceland; yet upon graduation, these players had to look elsewhere for the chance to play professionally. During Swedish coach Anna Signeul's tenure with the national team, and particularly as they moved towards their qualification campaign for the 2017 Women's European Championships, she encouraged the players to consider moving overseas to leagues where the standard of competition was more intense and the domestic set-up was better resourced and more professional. Scotland's top clubs began to move towards professionalisation in 2018, Northern Ireland's Premiership introduced some professional contracts in 2023, with Wales's Adran Premier alone remaining solely semi-professional ahead of the 2023/24 season, and some teams within that set-up still not paying their players at all. Female footballing hopefuls in Britain now may cast their eyes covetously only as far as England, rather than further afield as in previous generations, but carving out a career in the game at home remains a highly unlikely prospect.

It is also worth observing that even in the WSL set-up, prospects are far from perfect. Reading, relegated from the top division in 2023, withdrew from the second tier ahead of the 2024/25 season due to continuing financial difficulties. Manchester United hit the headlines in the summer of 2024 when it was announced that the women's squad would take up temporary residence in portable cabins at the club's training complex, with the men using the usual women's facilities while their own were refurbished. Though in recent years Arsenal have been playing frequently at the club's main stadium and attracting big crowds, London neighbours West Ham United have stuck to playing at their smaller ground in Dagenham, with a capacity of just over 6,000, stressing they would rather concentrate on growing their attendances more consistently.

In the summer of 2024, the Lionesses squad comprised players who competed domestically in the USA, Germany, France and Spain as well as England. With video, internet, international broadcasting deals and social media, few coaches now would object to their players pursuing a life abroad. Of course, these women now are all full-time, fully professional players, with agents, public relations teams, lawyers and more helping them when required; this generation are able to make decisions about their best footballing moves without anything else weighing in the balance. If they opt to play overseas, the media will run stories about it, breathlessly poring over the detail of the deal, the length of the contract, the transfer fee involved.

Yet as always when it comes to women's history, let alone women's football history, these moves abroad are nothing new. Though chances to make a fine living from the game might be recent developments, the chances taken by courageous women are not. Remember those who went before, took the risk, and flew the flag.

ACKNOWLEDGEMENTS

Thank you so much to the wonderful women who have spoken with me, several of whom then put me in touch with team-mates, friends and family who told me more about them. Many of these women are the players I grew up watching – in the case of Jeannie, a player who was almost mythical in her legendary status – and as always it's an honour to tell their stories. I particularly appreciate that some elements of their stories are sensitive or difficult to discuss, and I am so grateful for their honesty, their openness and their help.

Thank you also to those who watched and supported these women's careers in a variety of ways and spoke to me of their memories.

I should add that there are so many, many more female footballers who have played outside of the UK, in many different countries and for many different reasons, and I would have loved to have talked to every single one of them. This book is by necessity simply a snapshot of experiences. I should also add that I realise that the terms "Britain" and "British" can be politically charged and I have done my best to navigate this as sensitively as possible while retaining as clear a narrative as possible.

The nature of the research I have done for this book has meant translation of some original texts; thank you to those interviewees who have helped me with this. Any errors remaining are purely my own.

A special thank you to Elaine McHardy for sending me a selection of press cuttings and matchday programmes, invaluable to add some context around the Manchester footballing scene of the 1980s and 1990s, and to Vanessa O'Brien, for sharing some of her incredible hoard of memorabilia with me via airmail!

Thank you to Karen Farley, who over the past few years has been helpful above and beyond any reasonable expectation, and for this book trawled and shared her VHS collection of career highlights.

A huge thank you to Elsie Cook for her time and for collating so many other memories of Edna; I'm honoured to be able to piece together some of her remarkable life here.

Thank you to Janet Clark for putting me in touch with Jeannie; the original England team of 1972 have all been so wonderfully warm and welcoming to me and so open to telling their incredible stories and it's terrific to be able to add another chapter here; I feel very honoured to be able to put some of Jeannie's amazing life down on paper and to be able now to call her a friend.

I promised a thank you to the delightful Wilheminaboom bar and restaurant in beautiful Dordrecht, who welcomed me warmly and were fascinated to hear more about Jeannie; maybe we can have a book launch party now!

Thank you to Professor Fiona Skillen and Dr Karen Fraser for their huge support.

Professor Jean Williams's work on women's football history is fascinating and an invaluable grounding for anyone with an interest in the topic.

Thank you of course to my editor Christian Müller and the team at Hero, particularly Lucy Chamberlain and Olivia Le Maistre; thanks too to my agent Melanie Michael-Greer.

Finally, thank you to my husband Julian for his support, his driving, all the hot beverages, and never minding (too much) when he's told to keep quiet because I'm either on a call or transcribing one.

REFERENCES

Alderley and Wilmslow Advertiser (1966), 11th November 1966

Atria, 'The History of Dutch Women's Football', https://atria.nl/nieuws-publicaties/overig/vrouwen-in-sport/vrouwenvoetbal/

BBC, International Match of the Day, 13th June 1995

Chronicle, The (1966), 'Girl footballer as guest', 6th January, 1966

Dewar, Heather (2019), 'Rose Reilly says Scotland caps 'better late than never' after 1972 match against England; https://www.bbc.co.uk/sport/football/48426069

Campbell, Alan (2015), 'Death of a football trailblazer' https://www.heraldscotland.com/sport/13504711.death-football-trailblazer/

Cunningham, Sam (2022), 'Euro 2022: England's first women's team deserve an apology for being forgotten by the FA, claims former player' https://inews.co.uk/sport/football/euro-2022-england-first-womens-team-apology-forgotten-1762809

Evening Telegraph (1987), 'TV titbits', 7th January, 1987

Faller, Helge (2021), 'The Forgotten Pioneers', https://www.playingpasts.co.uk/articles/football/

the-forgotten-pioneers-international-womens-football-in-the-interwar-period-part-1/

Football Australia, 2023 Participation Report, https://www.footballaustralia.com.au/sites/ffa/files/2024-04/20488_FA_Participation%20Reports_2023_High%20Res.pdf

Football Australia, 2019 Participation Report, https://www.footballaustralia.com.au/sites/ffa/files/2020-03/2019%20National%20Participation%20Report-%20High%20Res.pdf

Hansard (1971), https://api.parliament.uk/historic-hansard/commons/1971/jan/28/average-weekly-wage

Hansard (1983), https://api.parliament.uk/historic-hansard/written-answers/1983/feb/10/average-weekly-wage

Harris, Nick, (2011) 'From £20 to £33,868 per week: a quick history of English football's top-flight wages' https://www.sportingintelligence.com/2011/01/20/from-20-to-33868-per-week-a-quick-history-of-english-footballs-top-flight-wages-200101/

Lawther, Steven (2021), 'Arrival: How Scotland's women took their place on the world stage and inspired a generation' (Pitch Publishing)

Lopez, Sue (1997), 'Women on the Ball: A guide to women's football' (Scarlet: London)

McFarlane, Bill (1977), 'Ally MacLeod doesn't know how lucky he is', Sunday Post, 29th May 1977

Middag, Tessel (2016), 'Football boots on her wishlist': The history of women's football in the Netherlands from 1880 to 1939 and the role of women in society (unpublished MA thesis)

National, The, 'Remembering Edna Neillis: A legend that many forgot' https://www.thenational.scot/sport/14853315. football-remembering-edna-neillis-a-legend-that-many-forgot/

Nutmeg, 'Scotland's most successful football export by a distance' https://www.nutmegmagazine.co.uk/issue-4/scotlands-most-successful-football-export-by-a-distance/

Rochdale Observer (1994), 'Striker hopes to spark a Welsh Euro revival', Saturday 12 March 1994

Scarborough Evening News (1989), 'Jane the England standard-raiser', 1st November, 1989

Scotsman, The, 'Edna Neillis: The Forgotten Pioneer of Women's Football' https://www.scotsman.com/news/edna-neillis-the-forgotten-pioneer-of-womens-football-3099786

Scottish FA, 'A History of Women's Football in Scotland' https://150.scottishfa.co.uk/scottish-football-history/a-history-of-womens-football-in-scotland/

Scottish Football Museum, 'Trailblazer Rose Reilly' https://www.scottishfootballmuseum.org.uk/news/trailblazer-rose-reilly/

Scottish Parliament, https://www.parliament.scot/chamber-and-committees/votes-and-motions/votes-and-motions-search/S4M-13934

Sentinel, The (1989), 'Kerry's England call', 28th September 1989

Sport Integrity Australia, 'Celebrating 100 years of women's soccer in Australia', https://www.sportintegrity.gov.au/news/integrity-blog/2021-09/celebrating-100-years-of-womens-soccer-australia

Sunday Post (1975), 'Luxury Life For Soccer Signorina', 17th August, 1975

Sunday Post (1983), 'Rose makes £700 a month – playing football!', 16th January, 1983

Williams, Jean, Globalising Women's Football